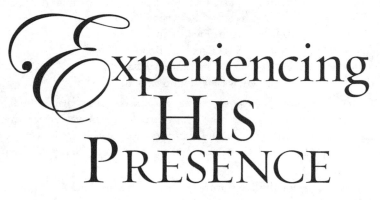

Experiencing His Presence

The Threshing Floor Devotional

Juanita Bynum

Charisma
HOUSE
A STRANG COMPANY

Most Strang Communications/Charisma House/Siloam/
FrontLine/Realms products are available at special quantity discounts for
bulk purchase for sales promotions, premiums, fund-raising, and educational
needs. For details, write Strang Communications/Charisma House/Siloam/
Realms, 600 Rinehart Road, Lake Mary, Florida 32746, or telephone (407)
333-0600.

Experiencing His Presence by Juanita Bynum
Published by Charisma House
A Strang Company
600 Rinehart Road
Lake Mary, Florida 32746
www.charismahouse.com

Unless otherwise noted, all Scripture quotations are from the Amplified Bible.
Old Testament © 1965, 1987 by the Zondervan Corporation. The Amplified
New Testament © 1954, 1958, 1987 by the Lockman Foundation. Used by
permission.

Scripture quotations marked KJV are from the King James Version of the Bible.

Scripture quotations marked NIV are from the Holy Bible, New International
Version, © 1973, 1978, 1984, International Bible Society. Used by permission.

Cover design by Bill Johnson
Interior design by Terry Clifton

Library of Congress Cataloging-in-Publication Data
Bynum, Juanita.
 Experiencing His presence / Juanita Bynum.
    p. cm.
 ISBN 1-59185-805-4 (casebound)
 1. Prayer--Christianity. I. Title.
 BV210.3.B96 2006
                        248.3'2--dc22
                                 2006020216

    06 07 08 09 10—987654321
    Printed in the United States of America

Introduction
A Journey Into His Presence

God established a tabernacle through His servant Moses so that the Israelites could understand how to come into His presence. Through the design of the tabernacle and the religious practices to be followed in the tabernacle, God illustrated what is required in order for us to be able to stand in His presence. The tabernacle demonstrates God's attributes and shows us how His blessings are made accessible to His people.

This book is a journey into the presence of the Lord. Through the tabernacle that was first established by God in the wilderness for the children of Israel, God's pattern and purpose for prayer will be revealed.

This book will also show you how the true meaning of the tabernacle has been distorted, even up to today. We have strayed far away from how God ordained that worship of Him was to be expressed.

In the following pages, I will break down major aspects of the tabernacle and create a pattern for you. When you have finished studying this pattern, you will be able to pray according to the pattern of the Lord wherever you are—at home in your bedroom or basement, in your car, or sitting in the pew at church.

Come with me; this journey is going to change your life for eternity.

Section 1

INTRODUCTION TO PRAYER

THE FIRST TABERNACLE

God designed the first tabernacle so that it was portable. He gave instructions for tearing it down, picking up the pieces, and moving it as the children of Israel went along their journey.

Every piece of that structure was sanctified and sacred, and the Israelites respected it. They knew that if they kept God's tabernacle in order, the presence of the Lord would lead them with a cloud by day and a fire by night. But every part of the tabernacle—from the doorposts to the ark of the covenant in the most holy place—had to be in order. No matter where they went on their journey, that order could not change.

The tabernacle held the very presence of God. It was the first time in history that God had come and dwelt among His people.

> Every part of the tabernacle— from the doorposts to the ark of the covenant in the most holy place—had to be in order.

Today His presence no longer dwells in a building; *God's people are the church,* and to hold the awesome presence of God Himself we must have lives that are in order according to the pattern He gave us when He provided instructions for the building of that first tabernacle. The pattern established for the Old Testament tabernacle is the spiritual pattern for you and me, who are the New Testament "temples of the Holy Spirit."

As the temple of the Holy Spirit, you must handle carefully the sacred pieces that you house, wherever you go and however you move. Anything that adversely affects those pieces will affect your relationship with God.

It isn't the *external* things people say about you or have done to you that affect your relationship with God. Your relationship with God is determined by how you handle or mishandle the *internal* pieces of the tabernacle that He has established within you.

Your relationship with God is determined by how you handle or mishandle the internal pieces of the tabernacle that He has established within you.

Do you not know that your body is a temple of the Holy Spirit, who is in you, whom you have received from God? You are not your own; you were bought at a price. Therefore honor God with your body.

—1 CORINTHIANS 6:19–20, NIV

THE PERFECT PATTERN

The pattern of the tabernacle was set forth for you to be able to see where you are in the realm of the Spirit and identify whatever may be in you that could hinder your prayers so that it can be corrected. God's desire is that our prayers would not be hindered. His desire is that it would not be a struggle for us to pray.

God doesn't want you to go to prayer shooting in the dark, not knowing if you are in His divine presence. He doesn't want you to have to wonder if He is hearing your prayers.

When you go to a tailor, he measures your body and then cuts out a pattern. The same is true with God's presence. If you don't pray according to the pattern He has cut, He will not be able to participate in your prayers. God can't commune with you on a human level—that pattern is too small.

God is sovereign. He can choose to answer an "out of pattern" prayer if He wants to. But in this last hour, God is bringing us a new confidence in prayer. As we learn to pray according to His pattern, we will see results—*every time.*

By the time you finish this book, you will be able to look back to times in the past when you have received answers from God, and you will recognize that the answers came because you prayed according to God's pattern—even without knowing it.

> God can't commune with you on a human level—that pattern is too small.

As we learn to pray according to His pattern, we will see results—every time.

So shall My word be that goes forth out of My mouth: it shall not return to Me void [without producing any effect, useless], but it shall accomplish that which I please and purpose, and it shall prosper in the thing for which I sent it.

—ISAIAH 55:11

THE GATE

*P*art of God's tabernacle construction plan was the erection of a wall of white linen, built to enclose the outer court. On the east side of this boundary was the entry gate.

The twelve tribes of Israel were camped around the outside of the wall. Each tribe had been given a specific location to pitch their tents. But each Israelite had to enter the tabernacle through the same gate. No one had special privileges and no one could slip under the curtain.

According to Exodus 27:16, multicolored curtains—blue, purple, and scarlet—were interwoven into this white linen gate. Each color represents a part of the work of Christ. White is His righteousness. Blue represents heaven. Purple stands for Jesus' royalty and kingship. Scarlet represents Jesus' ultimate sacrifice on the cross.

> Each Israelite had to enter the tabernacle through the same gate.

Today Jesus is the gate into the presence of God. Jesus stands between the things of God in the outer court and the world. To pass through the gate, you must accept Jesus as your Savior, and you must accept His works as part of your life.

As we approach the gate, Jesus stands there and says, "You don't know Me as your personal Savior. You are not saved. All that is behind Me within these courts are treasures of the will of My Father that you can freely have. I'm going to be your way in. You cannot skip this step...."

Today Jesus is the gate into the presence of God. Jesus stands between the things of God in the outer court and the world.

I am the door: by me if any man enter in, he shall be saved, and shall go in and out, and find pasture.... I am the way, the truth, and the life: no man cometh unto the Father, but by me.

—JOHN 10:9; 14:6, KJV

HAVE YOU RECEIVED CHRIST?

*I*f you are going to meet with God, you have to come through Jesus' works, which are represented by the gate. In other words, you have to be saved.

You have to receive Christ and acknowledge His works, or you won't even be able to get into the front yard—and forget about going behind the veil! If you haven't received Christ, that's out of the question. You can't come to the throne of God as a sinner—ignoring the works of the Son—and make intercession for somebody else. It can't happen; it breaks His pattern.

You can boldly approach God's throne, but only through the pattern of the finished, perfect works of Jesus Christ. When Jesus said, "I am the way, the truth, and the life" (John 14:6), He was marking the path to effective prayer. The gate is "the way"; the holy place (inner court) is "the truth"; and "the life" shines through God's perfected light in the most holy place.

You have to be saved. You have to be washed in the blood. God hears a sinner's prayer of repentance. (See Luke 5:32; Acts 2:21.) Your life cannot compare to the purity of the righteousness of God. But when you allow Jesus to become your righteousness, you can walk through the gate.

> The gate is "the way"; the holy place (inner court) is "the truth"; and "the life" shines through God's perfected light in the most holy place.

You have to receive Christ and acknowledge His works, or you won't even be able to get into the front yard.

Behold, the Lord's hand is not shortened at all, that it cannot save, nor His ear dull with deafness, that it cannot hear. But your iniquities have made a separation between you and your God, and your sins have hidden His face from you, so that He will not hear.

—ISAIAH 59:1–2

Jesus, the Perfect High Priest

In the Old Testament, God chose and qualified the priests according to the Law that He had revealed to Moses. The priests worked hard to keep themselves consecrated according to this Law. Their very lives depended on it. But even though they worked hard to fulfill all the requirements of the Law, they could not attain perfection. In Aaron's priestly order, the priests would ultimately die because they were human.

Jesus' priesthood is different. It didn't come from the order of man, but from the third realm, where God dwells in eternal light. Jesus was with the Father before the foundation of the world. (See John 1:1–2.) As a priest, Jesus didn't *officiate* at the altar. *He climbed up on the altar and became the sacrifice.* He went into the fire. He has one goal: to give us a living, breathing, vital relationship with the Father.

That relationship enables you to become an effective intercessor, because if you can believe it for yourself, then you can believe it on behalf of someone else.

When you enter the gate, you are thanking God for providing a perfect Priest. You have acknowledged His works, understanding that He has saved you to the uttermost.

Besides that, Jesus Christ, the perfect High Priest, forever lives to make intercession for you and me. He never stops praying!

> As a priest, Jesus didn't *officiate* at the altar. *He climbed up on the altar and became the sacrifice.*

If you can believe it for yourself, then you can believe it on behalf of someone else.

He [Jesus] holds His priesthood unchangeably, because He lives on forever. Therefore He is able also to save to the uttermost (completely, perfectly, finally, and for all time and eternity).

—Hebrews 7:24–25

The Power of the Gate

The first gate sets the groundwork for the rest of your journey. The *gate,* the *outer court,* the *door,* the *holy place,* the *veil,* and the *most holy place* work together in prayer. So if you ignore the works of Christ in the gate, you could delay or abort other things God has already provided for you in prayer.

If you neglect this first gate, you will have neglected an act of God, which can negate a prayer He wants to answer before you ask. The Bible says that God knows what you need even "before you ask Him" (Matt. 6:8). For example, before you asked Jesus into your heart, God was already wooing and drawing you to the gate. God provided for your salvation before you asked Jesus to save your soul.

> The *gate,* the *outer court,* the *door,* the *holy place,* the veil, and the *most holy place* work together in prayer.

There is no shortcut to effective prayer. At each entry—the gate, the door, and the veil—you must travel the same path: *Jesus.* At every level of prayer and intercession, Jesus is the only way to true communion with God.

Take some time at this gate. Make sure you really know Jesus and understand exactly what He has done for you—because once you walk into the court, God is going to take you to victory.

At each entry—the gate, the door, and the veil—Jesus is the only way to true communion with God.

When you pray, do not be like the hypocrites, for they love to pray standing in the synagogues and on the street corners to be seen by men....But when you pray, go into your room, close the door and pray to your Father, who is unseen....And when you pray, do not keep on babbling like pagans, for they think they will be heard because of their many words. Do not be like them, for your Father knows what you need before you ask him.

—Matthew 6:5–8, niv

Section 2

THE EARLY STAGES OF PRAYER

MOVING FORWARD

*G*od is always moving forward. So when you walk into the outer court of prayer, He wants you to keep moving forward, too. You have entered God's presence through the gate of Jesus Christ, yet He wants you to go deeper.

Outer court prayer is the first stage of prayer. It corresponds to your initial conversion experience, and it sets the groundwork for you in the Spirit realm, allowing God to continue to build on that foundation.

Anyone who has received Jesus can come into the outer court. It is a place of washing and repentance—a place we enter with thanksgiving for what He has done.

Many people enter the courts of the Lord, embrace religion, and never go deeper into God's presence. He wants to lead us through the outer court into the holy place, and then finally into the most holy place, where we will experience His glory and bring it back into the earthly realm. We must obey Him at every step to keep making progress.

> Outer court prayer is the first stage of prayer. It corresponds to your initial conversion experience.

God wants to lead us through the outer court into the holy place, and then finally into the most holy place, where we will experience His glory and bring it back into the earthly realm. We must obey Him at every step to keep making progress.

Someone asked him, "Lord, are only a few people going to be saved?" He said to them, "Make every effort to enter through the narrow door, because many, I tell you, will try to enter and will not be able to."

—LUKE 13:23–24, NIV

The Outer Court

The people of Israel gathered in the outer court. They discussed their opinions about God and other things—and it kept them from getting closer to Him. When the Israelites "murmured," complaining to each other about what they thought God was doing, their murmurings delayed their progress. (See Exodus 15:24.) Circumstances and relationships worsened. Judgment followed.

Outer court chatter will hinder your prayers! It's OK to enjoy your new spiritual family, but keep pressing toward God.

> When you stay in the outer court, you stay focused on *what you need* instead of on *who you are in Christ.*

Every believer can walk into the outer court. Everyone can pray in the name of Jesus. But outer court pray-ers are inconsistent. They pray *whenever*. They cry out to God in emergencies. They may also stay in praise mode, admiring God but never coming into a relationship with Him so they can learn what is on His heart.

Outer court pray-ers never get to the stage where they declare, "Thy kingdom come." Instead, they say, "I'm saved." Now, coming through the gate of Christ is a wonderful blessing. Acknowledging God as your Provider, Peace, Righteousness, Banner of Protection, and so on is even better. However, when you stay in the outer court, you stay focused on *what you need* instead of on *who you are in Christ.*

Outer court chatter will hinder your prayers.

Brethren, my heart's desire and prayer to God for Israel is, that they might be saved. For I bear them record that they have a zeal of God, but not according to knowledge. For they being ignorant of God's righteousness, and going about to establish their own righteousness, have not submitted themselves unto the righteousness of God.

—Romans 10:1–3, KJV

BY NATURAL LIGHT

The outer court was lit by natural sunlight.

Believers in the outer court are still under the influence of natural light. Even though they are saved, they are constantly being exposed to natural elements.

In the outer court stage of prayer you see people who are crippled, sick, and depressed in spite of their prayers for healing, deliverance, and peace. This is because a believer can't pray effectually in the outer court. Effectual prayers are the result of passing through to maturity by surrender to God.

The outer court is a wonderful place, but it only stays wonderful as long as you are passing through. You must move on to maturity, which is found at the brazen laver and the brazen altar in the heart of the outer court.

The outer court person who approaches the brazen laver to be washed clean becomes the intercessor who maintains the holy place, keeping the temple in order. This person then enters the most holy place, where tremendous power is available, dynamic in its working. This person then becomes a fully matured, consecrated intercessor.

You aren't supposed to stay under the influence of natural light, praying only what you can see in the natural. God wants you to pray by divine revelation, which comes only from Him in the most holy place.

> The outer court is a wonderful place, but it only stays wonderful as long as you are passing through. You must move on to maturity.

Even though believers in the outer court are saved, they are constantly being exposed to natural elements.

Therefore let us go on and get past the elementary stage in the teachings and doctrine of Christ (the Messiah), advancing steadily toward the completeness and perfection that belong to spiritual maturity. Let us not again be laying the foundation of repentance and abandonment of dead works (dead formalism) and of the faith [by which you turned] to God.

—HEBREWS 6:1

NOT OF THIS WORLD

When a person is assigned to serve as a United States ambassador in a remote, impoverished country in Africa, the community around the new ambassador may be impoverished, but the U.S. embassy furnishes him with a Mercedes Benz and one of the most beautiful houses you have ever seen. Why?

Because although the ambassador and his family live in Africa, they are not citizens of that country. They are citizens of the United States of America, and as such they may enjoy the kind of lifestyle to which they would be entitled in this country. This isn't merely for their comfort; it is also so that others can look at their lifestyle and see a picture of America.

> God has prepared great things for those who love and seek after Him with all their hearts.

God has prepared great things for those who love and seek after Him with all their hearts. The outer court is just the beginning. Moving beyond it, we can become ambassadors for Christ. Our lifestyle—the way we carry ourselves and the way we live—must exemplify our heavenly citizenship.

As an ambassador for Christ, you will be able to take help from heaven and distribute it to those who live in a place that is remote from His kingdom. This is true intercession.

Moving beyond the outer court, we can become ambassadors for Christ.

"No eye has seen, no ear has heard, no mind has conceived what God has prepared for those who love him"—but God has revealed it to us by his Spirit.

—1 CORINTHIANS 2:9–10, NIV

PRAYING LIKE ELIJAH

The Old Testament prophet Elijah knew how to enter into the realm of divine revelation, intervention, strength, and power. He was an ordinary person like you or me, yet he was able to move beyond his natural flesh—consistently. Not only was Elijah able to stop the rain from falling, but he also had power with God to restore it again.

He was able to control the weather through his prayers because he prayed so faithfully. What an amazing example of a true ambassador in prayer.

God makes this same level of power available to anyone who passes through the outer court into the holy place. Yes, even *you* can alter the course of nature or change lives! God will do powerful things through you as He did through Elijah, if you respect and follow the pattern.

You might be thinking, *I've been saved from sin, but it still looks glamorous to me. I just keep slipping back into it.* Hear me. As long as you keep slipping back, you will never move on to maturity. You will never become an effectual intercessor. You don't have to settle for the outer court; God wants to help you move forward.

> Elijah was an ordinary person like you or me, yet he was able to move beyond his natural flesh—consistently.

God will do powerful things through you as He did through Elijah, if you respect and follow the pattern.

Elijah was a human being with a nature such as we have [with feelings, affections, and a constitution like ours]; and he prayed earnestly for it not to rain, and no rain fell on the earth for three years and six months. And [then] he prayed again and the heavens supplied rain and the land produced its crops [as usual].

—JAMES 5:17–18

A Glimpse of Glory

hough we pass through the processes of outer court prayer (cleansing) and holy place prayer (maintenance), God has not declared that He will meet with us in either of those places. It is in the third place of prayer, between the cherubim on the mercy seat, that God declared, "There…I will meet with you" (Exod. 25:22).

> You can experience the presence of God when you are in the outer court, but that doesn't mean you have entered into intercession.

You can experience the presence of God when you are in the outer court, but that doesn't mean you have entered into intercession. Actually, you are only feeling the residue of His glory, which is emanating from the most holy place.

In Old Testament days, when the high priest offered up the most holy perfume to God on the altar of incense, the scent of that offering went throughout the tent of meeting. Some of it escaped into the outer court. Even today, people in the outer court smell the incense of the Lord. But there is more.

Though you are saved and in the outer court, God is calling you to a deeper level of prayer. Follow Him. Pass through every level, every piece of furniture in the tabernacle, to enter the third realm of intercession. This is the place from which you can change the course of this world as a result of your intercessory prayers.

Press past the sweet aroma to the place where God will meet with you in His glory. Don't get stuck in the outer court. Don't be satisfied with just a glimpse, only an aroma of God's glorious presence.

Don't be satisfied with just a glimpse, only an aroma of God's glorious presence.

May my prayer be set before you like incense; may the lifting up of my hands be like the evening sacrifice. Set a guard over my mouth, O LORD; keep watch over the door of my lips. Let not my heart be drawn to what is evil, to take part in wicked deeds with men who are evildoers; let me not eat of their delicacies.

—PSALM 141:2–4, NIV

Section 3

THE PLACE OF WASHING

THE BRAZEN LAVER

*Y*ou have passed through the gate that represents the four works of Jesus Christ: His righteousness, divinity, kingship, and ultimate sacrifice on the cross. These four works of Christ allow you to enter His courts in prayer. You have kept moving forward through the outer court, drawing ever nearer to God.

Now you are about to come to the place where you will become a *reflection of Christ.* In the Old Testament tabernacle, this place was called the brazen laver. The laver is the first piece of furniture in the tabernacle.

> You are about to come to the place where you will become a *reflection of Christ.*

The brazen laver is a place of sanctification. It is where the Word of God cleanses you and begins to prepare you to serve in your priestly function as an intercessor. Just as it is the first piece of furniture in the old tabernacle, it is the first aspect of God's nature that embraces your life.

The outer court person who approaches the brazen laver to wash now becomes the intercessor who can move into the holy place.

The brazen laver is a place of sanctification, where the Word of God cleanses you and begins to prepare you to serve in your priestly function as an intercessor.

Then the LORD said to Moses, "Make a bronze basin, with its bronze stand, for washing. Place it between the Tent of Meeting and the altar, and put water in it. Aaron and his sons are to wash their hands and feet with water from it. Whenever they enter the Tent of Meeting, they shall wash with water so that they will not die. Also, when they approach the altar to minister by presenting an offering made to the Lord by fire, they shall wash their hands and feet so that they will not die."

—EXODUS 30:17–21, NIV

A Royal Priesthood

Every priest was required to wash before performing any ministry. By washing their hands and feet, the priests were demonstrating their total devotion to God's service.

So what does this have to do with you? You have come into the outer court by receiving a personal relationship with Jesus. But now God wants you to keep moving forward. He wants you to pass through the personal level of prayer (through washing at the laver) in order to prepare you to pray for others.

You have already tasted the goodness of God through salvation at the gate. Now you must let Him build His character in you. This is how He prepares you to do His work. The work of prayer has been given to each and every believer. It doesn't matter how old you are in Christ—God has called you to pray every day.

> Now you must let Him build His character in you.

Since prayer is not just a personal relationship with God, but also a ministry, before you can minister on any level—to yourself, to someone else, or to the Lord—you must first wash at the laver. This cleansing prepares you to minister.

If you're thinking, *I'm not a priest,* think again. When you received Christ, you did not merely become a part of God's family—you became a part of His royal priesthood. This new work of the priesthood begins within you at the brazen laver.

Before you can minister on any level—to yourself, to someone else, or to the Lord—you must first wash at the laver. This cleansing prepares you to minister.

So be done with every trace of wickedness (depravity, malignity) and all deceit and insincerity (pretense, hypocrisy) and grudges (envy, jealousy) and slander and evil speaking of every kind.…[Come] and, like living stones, be yourselves built [into] a spiritual house, for a holy (dedicated, consecrated) priesthood, to offer up [those] spiritual sacrifices [that are] acceptable and pleasing to God through Jesus Christ.

—1 Peter 2:1, 5

A PURE BRIDE

As a member of the bride of Christ, every believer must undergo a cleansing process. As soon as you come into the outer court, Christ leads you straight to the brazen laver, because He has already given Himself up as a holy sacrifice to make you righteous.

In practical terms, Jesus gave up His life to sanctify you "by the washing of water with the Word" (Eph. 5:26). Washing in the Word helps you to strip off the "old (unregenerate) self," which is your flesh (Col. 3:9). Until you wash at the brazen laver, you live "according to the flesh and are controlled by its unholy desires" (Rom. 8:5).

In the outer court, you are still setting your mind on the things that gratify your flesh. If you live by the flesh, you will "surely die," but if you are cleansed at the brazen laver, "through the power of the [Holy] Spirit you are [habitually] putting to death (making extinct, deadening) the [evil] deeds prompted by the body," and "you shall [really and genuinely] live forever" (Rom. 8:13). Our sanctification at the brazen laver is the work of the Holy Spirit. "He is the Life-giver" (John 6:63).

> Jesus Christ has already given Himself up as a holy sacrifice to make you righteous.

Even though you are a believer, unless you submit to the washing of the Spirit at the brazen laver, you will be controlled by your lower nature. God can't use a fleshly intercessor. When the Old Testament priests performed daily sacrifices, they burned the animal skins (the outer flesh) outside the camp. (See Leviticus 8; 9.) There's no room for your flesh in prayer! You must wash at the laver to get cleansed and prepared for the next level of consecration.

Unless you submit to the washing of the Spirit at the brazen laver, you will be controlled by your lower nature.

Christ loved the church and gave Himself up for her, so that He might sanctify her, having cleansed her by the washing of water with the Word, that He might present the church to Himself in glorious splendor, without spot or wrinkle or any such things [that she might be holy and faultless].

—EPHESIANS 5:25–27

A PERFECT CONSTRUCTION

*I*n general the Old Testament tabernacle furniture was constructed from wood (which represents humanity) and then overlaid with either copper or gold. Some items were solid gold or copper.

The brazen laver was made of solid copper (translated as "bronze" or "brass" in some Bible versions). (See Exodus 30:17–21). Copper symbolizes *God's judgment*. It reminds us that He is the final judge of whether or not we are spiritually clean. Washing at the laver should also remind us that there is a final judgment for those who reject the Word. (See John 3:18; Revelation 20:11–15.)

The meaning is clear: *we must not reject the cleansing.*

As your Lord, Jesus is able to begin transforming you into the image of God. You can't do this for yourself. Only Jesus can. I believe this is why the laver had no recorded measurements and no wood used in its construction. The Word of God is absolutely *unlimited* in its ability to wash and cleanse you!

Nothing is too deep within you for Jesus' laver to reach, too far back in your past for Him to erase, or too distant into your future for Him to control. The cleansing power of the laver is unlimited, so you can become exactly who God has destined you to be in His kingdom.

> The brazen laver was made of solid copper, which symbolizes *God's judgment*. It reminds us that He is the final judge of whether we are spiritually clean.

The Word of God is absolutely unlimited *in its ability to wash and cleanse you!*

You have come to God, the judge of all men, to the spirits of righteous men made perfect, to Jesus the mediator of a new covenant, and to the sprinkled blood that speaks a better word than the blood of Abel.

—HEBREWS 12:23–24, NIV

A Perfect Reflection

*I*n Old Testament days, the mirrors that women used were made from polished bronze. We know that the brazen laver was formed from the mirrors of the Israelite women who served at the entrance of the tent of the tabernacle. (See Exodus 38:8.)

When a priest approached the polished bronze basin to wash, he would see his reflection in the water. He would also see a second reflection of his face in the bowl of the basin itself. There could be no mistake about how he looked.

In the same way, when you go to the brazen laver in prayer, God shows you a true reflection of who you are in the natural. He also gives you a glimpse of who you are becoming as He imparts the Word into your life. This is His process of "completing" your salvation. (See 1 Peter 2:1–5.)

When you decide to go ahead and let Him wash you, you dip your hands into the basin. Now you are *doing* the Word, and your response enables God to impart to you from the basin. You become clean again, and your new reflection shows it.

This is the twofold power of the brazen laver. It shows you what you look like—before and after—and it cleanses you.

> When a priest approached the polished bronze basin to wash, he would see his reflection in the water, and he would also see a second reflection of his face in the bowl of the basin itself.

The twofold power of the brazen laver shows you what you look like—before and after—and it cleanses you.

They made the bronze basin and its bronze stand from the mirrors of the women who served at the entrance to the Tent of Meeting.

—Exodus 38:8, NIV

SUBMIT TO THE WASHING

*L*et's talk more about *doing* the Word.

Many people hear the Word but fail to understand that they need to *do* what it says. They hang around in the outer court. After a while, they may wander over to the brazen laver to wash. But to tell the truth, it's only because everybody else is doing it. Once they get up to the basin, they can't endure the washing process, so they run off to a corner where they feel more comfortable. Then they wonder why God doesn't seem to answer their prayers. They think that God is just *supposed* to answer their prayers, even though they constantly break His pattern.

If only they would take a minute to look at their reflection in the laver! By reflecting the Word into their hearts, it would reveal the truth about who they really are. When they see their condition reflected in the laver, they would understand right away that the cleansing process isn't just some kind of a religious obligation; it's a primary *need*. We all *need* to be washed.

When we behold ourselves in the water of the Word, the next step is easy—reaching into the water to become sanctified from sin and iniquity. We can't go deeper in God until we are washed and sanctified at the brazen laver.

> People think that God is just *supposed* to answer their prayers, even though they constantly break His pattern.

We can't go deeper in God until we are washed and sanctified at the brazen laver.

Now ye are clean through the word which I have spoken unto you.

—JOHN 15:3, KJV

A Perfect Communion

When we wash at the brazen laver (when we pray daily), we come into communion with Jesus Christ, our High Priest. We discover that our Father brings "many sons into glory" and brings "to maturity the human experience necessary to be perfectly equipped" (Heb. 2:10). At the laver, the washing of the Word sanctifies us and prepares us for the work of an intercessor.

> We are a royal priesthood, and as often as we do our priestly duty of prayer (every day), remembering Him, we share communion with Him.

We are a royal priesthood, joint heirs with Christ, so we must move through every stage of prayer by way of His sacrifice. Like the bread and wine of Communion, Jesus' body was broken and His blood was shed so that we could walk in new life with Him. Therefore, as often as we do our priestly duty of prayer (every day), remembering Him, we share communion with Him. We reaffirm our love, trust, and commitment to Him, and He transforms us into the image of God by the mighty power of His Word. In this way we demonstrate the works that He has already accomplished. (See 1 Corinthians 11:26.)

At the gate, we *acknowledge* His works. At the laver, we begin to *demonstrate* them.

At the gate, we acknowledge His works. At the laver, we begin to demonstrate them.

For the Word that God speaks is alive and full of power [making it active, operative, energizing, and effective]; it is sharper than any two-edged sword, penetrating to the dividing line of the breath of life (soul) and [the immortal] spirit, and of joints and marrow [of the deepest parts of our nature], exposing and sifting and analyzing and judging the very thoughts and purposes of the heart.... Inasmuch then as we have a great High Priest Who has [already] ascended and passed through the heavens, Jesus the Son of God, let us hold fast our confession [of faith in Him].

—Hebrews 4:12, 14

You Cannot Stay at the Laver

Though you need to wash at the brazen laver, you cannot remain there. When you are there, you are still in the outer court level of prayer, so the only person you will be able to pray for is yourself. Remember, outer court prayer focuses on *self*—*your* wrongdoings, *your* limitations and failures, what *you* need to overcome, and so on. At this stage, it's all about *you*.

As a matter of fact, the priests themselves could not remain at the laver for very long each day before they started performing their priestly duties. Like the Old Testament priests, we should submit to the process and become thoroughly clean, but not take too long doing it. Let the Word do a quick work in you.

As the priests washed at the brazen laver daily, so you should wash in the Word every single day. You can't wash one day and skip the next. Priests couldn't skip days in performing their duties. After they became priests, they remained as such for the rest of their time on Earth. It's the same with us.

Failing to wash yourself in the living Word of God means you are bypassing the work of your Savior and trying to come to God on your own merits. Remember, Jesus said, "I am the Way and the Truth and the Life; no one comes to the Father except by (through) Me" (John 14:6). If you skip the Way, you definitely have not arrived at the Truth, and you certainly have not reached the Life.

You cannot have a successful, effective prayer life without the Word of God.

> As the priests washed at the brazen laver daily, so you should wash in the Word every single day. You can't wash one day and skip the next.

Failing to wash yourself in the living Word of God means you are bypassing the work of your Savior and trying to come to God on your own merits.

I call to you, O Lord, every day; I spread out my hands to you.... But I cry to you for help, O Lord; in the morning my prayer comes before you.

—Psalm 88:9, 13, niv

Section 4

THE PLACE OF SACRIFICE

THE BRAZEN ALTAR

*L*et's review. You have entered prayer through the gate of Jesus Christ, with thanksgiving and praise for what He has done. You have drawn near to God by moving through every distraction in the outer court. You have submitted to the "washing of the Word" at the brazen laver, and now you know exactly what "manner of man" you are. The transformation has begun.

Because you have now washed at the brazen laver, it is time to be purified at the brazen altar. This is the second stage within the outer court. The brazen altar is where you will let go of your selfish determinations and embrace everything the Lord wants to do in your life.

Immature (infant believer) prayer always says, "Give me this. Give me that." But the mature prayer of sacrifice says, "God, I surrender to *Your* will. I want whatever *You* want." The brazen altar stage says yes to God.

After the way (the gate) and the truth (the brazen laver) you come to the altar, where you will find that your "death" leads to *life*. In order for the way and the truth to lead you into new life, you have to go through a death on the brazen altar of God's tabernacle. There is fire on that altar, but it isn't a destructive flame; it's a constructive one. Though this fire gets rid of the bad elements, it allows that which remains to be formed and shaped until it adheres completely to God's image.

> Because you have now washed at the brazen laver, it is time to be purified at the brazen altar.

The mature prayer of sacrifice says yes to God: "God, I surrender to Your will. I want whatever You want."

And thou shalt burn the whole ram upon the altar: it is a burnt offering unto the LORD: it is a sweet savour, an offering made by fire unto the LORD.

—EXODUS 29:18, KJV

WHAT IS AN ALTAR?

*S*acrifice always comes before service. Many people think they are serving God in the sanctuary—preaching, praying, prophesying—but they haven't been to the brazen altar! They haven't stopped at the place of sacrifice to give everything to God. *They are still controlled by their own will.*

In Hebrew, the word *altar* means "a slaughter place." In Greek, it means "a place of sacrifice." The brazen altar is the place where the natural, earthly things that hinder your walk with God are consumed by the fire of God. On the altar, you become a living sacrifice. You surrender your will to your Lord.

Having become a member of the royal priesthood of Jesus Christ, you must wash yourself first and then undergo the fire of consecration. Otherwise you will not be qualified for true ministry. You must prove the new ideals and attitude you received at the brazen laver by laying down your life to embrace God's perfect will. The consuming fire of God's Holy Spirit will draw out everything within you that does not line up with God's perfect will.

It's similar to the process of forging gold. The goldsmith puts the gold into the fire to draw out the impurities. As they come to the surface, he scrapes them off and then puts the gold back into the flames. He does this repeatedly until that piece of gold is pure right down to its deepest interior part.

As fiery trials come our way, let's cooperate with the Spirit, releasing the impurities that rise up within us. What is our goal? To become valuable to God, pure to the core.

> The word *altar* means "a slaughter place" or "a place of sacrifice." The brazen altar is the place where the natural, earthly things that hinder your walk with God are consumed by the fire of God.

Everything within you that does not line up with God's perfect will shall be set on fire and consumed by the Spirit.

I appeal to you therefore, brethren, and beg of you in view of [all] the mercies of God, to make a decisive dedication of your bodies [presenting all your members and faculties] as a living sacrifice, holy (devoted, consecrated) and well pleasing to God, which is your reasonable (rational, intelligent) service and spiritual worship.

—ROMANS 12:1

A SOUND CONSTRUCTION

The brazen altar was formed out of wood and then overlaid in copper ("brass" or "bronze" in some Bible translations). Wood represents humanity, and whenever humanity is involved, there will be limitations. But because copper symbolizes judgment, the brazen altar is where God atones for the limitations of man through the shedding of blood.

God specified the exact size of the altar. He told Moses to make it "five cubits square and three cubits high [within reach of all]" (Exod. 27:1). Five symbolizes *grace,* and three represents the three-in-one Godhead: Father, Son, and Holy Spirit. Thus the brazen altar is where the grace of the Godhead transforms whoever will become a living sacrifice.

God has already tempered and perfected the altar fire to match each and every person who will enter it. No two people go through the same trials. God's well-tempered flames burn up only what He cannot use. They will not consume any part of you that He desires to use.

> The brazen altar is where the grace of the Godhead transforms whoever will become a living sacrifice.

On the four corners of this altar, God specified that four horns should be formed, overlaid with bronze so as to be of one piece with the altar. We will talk more about these horns later. God also directed Moses to make bronze pots for the ashes, and bronze utensils such as shovels, basins, forks, and firepans. He spelled out how each additional item should look: a grate, a network of bronze with four bronze rings at the corners, and carrying poles of acacia wood overlaid with more bronze.

A brazen altar—wood overlaid with bronze—represents our humanness overlaid and beautified with the fire-purified precious grace.

God has already tempered and perfected the altar fire to match each and every person who will enter it. No two people go through the same trials.

For even to this were you called.... For Christ also suffered for you, leaving you [His personal] example, so that you should follow in His footsteps.

—1 PETER 2:21

THY WILL BE DONE

*I*n the Garden of Gethsemane, Jesus prayed until "His sweat became like great clots of blood dropping down upon the ground" (Luke 22:44). He laid down His will and said, "Father, if You are willing, remove this cup from Me; yet not My will, but [always] Yours be done" (v. 42). At this moment in the realm of the Spirit, Jesus had made it to the brazen altar. He lay before His Father God and declared, "In My flesh, I don't want to do this. I cannot do this. Nevertheless, I want whatever You want. Yes, Father!"

You must make the same transaction. Before you can operate in the Spirit realm, you must stop at the brazen altar to lay down your own will. Jesus is already there before you with His amazing grace. He will bring you through the fire.

Let go of your will. Put yourself on the brazen altar, and God will lead you to the second and third realms in prayer. You won't carry your thoughts, ways, and ideas to His throne— instead you will receive divine knowledge and revelation from Him as to how you should pray. This is why you must go beyond outer court prayer.

> You must stop at the brazen altar to lay down your own will. Jesus is already there before you with His amazing grace. He will bring you through the fire.

Put yourself on the brazen altar, and God will lead you to the second and third realms in prayer.

For we do not have a High Priest Who is unable to understand and sympathize and have a shared feeling with our weaknesses and infirmities and liability to the assaults of temptation, but One Who has been tempted in every respect as we are, yet without sinning.

—HEBREWS 4:15

An Equal Sacrifice

The brazen altar was three cubits high, which symbolized the Godhead. It matched the height of the ark of the covenant, which was kept behind the veil in the most holy place. (The base of the ark was two and a half cubits, but it became three cubits if you included the height of the cherubim on the cover.)

I believe these matching measurements indicate that the glory of God will be equal to the sacrifice that is made on the brazen altar. If you have no communion with God at the altar, you won't have a match or connection with God in the most holy place. Your sacrifice must measure up to the level of glory you want to experience with God in intercession.

Too many believers want great power with little or no sacrifice. They want to experience deep prayer in the most holy place, but they don't want to give up living in sin. They will never get to the most holy place, because they are disregarding God's pattern.

> These matching measurements indicate that the glory of God will be equal to the sacrifice that is made on the brazen altar.

The apostle Paul wrote about this balance of sacrifice and glory in the fifth and sixth chapters of his letter to the Roman believers. He wrote, "We were buried therefore with Him by the baptism into death *[at the brazen altar of prayer],* so that just as Christ was raised from the dead by the glorious [power] of the Father, so we too might [habitually] live and behave in newness of life *[before the ark of the covenant]*" (Rom. 6:4).

Wood, which represents humanity, kept the altar fire burning. In other words, God requires us to lay ourselves on the brazen altar every day. We are the wood that keeps God's altar fire burning.

God requires us to lay ourselves on the brazen altar every day. We are the wood that keeps God's altar fire burning.

For if we have become one with Him by sharing a death like His, we shall also be [one with Him in sharing] His resurrection [by a new life lived for God].

—Romans 6:5

HORNS OF HELP

God doesn't expect you to sacrifice yourself without His help. He has provided for you by putting four horns on the corners of the brazen altar. They represent *salvation, strength,* and *power.* After you lay hold of the strength and power of your salvation, you can lay down on the altar everything that is in your mind and heart.

Never forget the salvation that Jesus has won for you. You must approach the altar on God's terms, by means of Jesus' blood sacrifice, which purchased your salvation.

Also, remember that there are four horns on the altar. The number four represents the earth and its elements—the four winds and the four corners of the earth (the four compass directions). This shows us that Christ's power to help you in prayer is unlimited; it extends to all four corners of the earth.

When you embrace the fullness of God's provision at the altar of sacrifice, you are fully able to relinquish your sinful impurities and willful human limitations. You can rise up in the power of the Holy Spirit—to pray as Jesus does.

> The four horns on the corners of the brazen altar represent God's unlimited salvation, strength, and power.

Christ's power to help you in prayer is unlimited; it extends to all four corners of the earth.

Blessed (praised and extolled and thanked) be the Lord, the God of Israel, because He has come and brought deliverance and redemption to His people! And He has raised up a Horn of salvation [a mighty and valiant Helper, the Author of salvation] for us in the house of David His servant.

—LUKE 1:68–69

WORK OUT YOUR SALVATION

The judgment of God will begin "with the household of God…it begins with us." Peter asks the question, "What will [be] the end of those who do not respect or believe or obey the good news (the Gospel) of God? And if the righteous are barely saved, what will become of the godless and wicked?" (1 Pet. 4:17–18).

It is so important that we recognize our need to work out our own salvation at the brazen altar, fearing God and honoring Christ's sacrifice. We cannot remain passive; we need to make ourselves do it. We must take hold of our full salvation. If we don't actively work out our salvation, we will be stuck in the outer court.

Only because we have been saved in Jesus' name can we lie on the altar and complete the process of purification. Trusting Him in the purifying fire strengthens our faith to do His works and enables us to pray for others. When we make intercession and God answers our prayers, we won't become proud and forget the name that put the horns of salvation, strength, and power on the altar of sacrifice.

Unless we have consistently worked out our own salvation through faith in Christ on the altar, we will not have the faith to pray for others. It is the man and woman whose faith has made them just and upright who will be able also to live—every day—by faith. (See Romans 1:17.)

> It is so important that we recognize our need to work out our own salvation at the brazen altar, fearing God and honoring Christ's sacrifice. We cannot remain passive.

Trusting Him in the purifying fire strengthens our faith to do His works and enables us to pray for others.

Therefore, my dear friends, as you have always obeyed—not only in my presence, but now much more in my absence—continue to work out your salvation with fear and trembling, for it is God who works in you to will and to act according to his good purpose.

—PHILIPPIANS 2:12–13, NIV

Salvation Defeats the Enemy

When you take hold of the horns of the altar, you receive the help you need to lay down your will and receive completed salvation. The Holy Spirit, who is your Helper, makes it possible. This Helper is going to be with you at every level of prayer and intercession.

All through the Bible, we see examples of how completed salvation defeats the enemy. Remember Joshua and the walls of Jericho? The children of Israel marched around the city and blew a ram's horn (which represents salvation) in obedience to God's command. At the sound of the horn the people raised a great shout, and the city walls fell to the ground.

> The Holy Spirit, who is your Helper, is going to be with you at every level of prayer and intercession.

Remember when God told Abraham to sacrifice his son Isaac on an altar? Abraham obeyed, and at the last minute God provided a ram to kill instead of his son. By means of his willing sacrifice, Abraham was qualified to become the "father of many nations" (Gen. 17:4).

We see a literal example in the story of King David and his sons, Adonijah and Solomon. King David was old, and he wanted Solomon to become the next king. But Adonijah seized the throne. When David found out, Adonijah ran to the tabernacle and grabbed hold of the horns of the altar for protection. God honored His provision of protection, and although Solomon was destined to become the king, Adonijah's life was spared.

When you take hold of the horns of the altar, you receive the help you need to lay down your will and receive completed salvation.

> But Adonijah, in fear of Solomon, went and took hold of the horns of the altar. Then Solomon was told, "Adonijah is afraid of King Solomon and is clinging to the horns of the altar." ...Solomon replied, "If he shows himself to be a worthy man, not a hair of his head will fall to the ground; but if evil is found in him, he will die." Then King Solomon sent men, and they brought him down from the altar. And Adonijah came and bowed down to King Solomon, and Solomon said, "Go to your home."
>
> —1 Kings 1:50–53, niv

BEWARE OF STRANGE FIRE

*O*nly the fire of God is worthy to be used in His tabernacle. There is no place for strange fire to be brought in from another source.

What do I mean by "strange fire"? The sons of Aaron (Nadab and Abihu) offered unholy fire before the Lord, and they lost their lives as a result of their actions. They refused to submit to God's pattern. In a similar way, if you don't lay down your own will on the brazen altar before you minister, you are lighting a strange fire.

Strange fires can be seen everywhere in Christendom today. They have been lit by people who have remained enslaved to their flesh while trying to serve the Lord. These people have bypassed the altar of sacrifice in favor of doing whatever they prefer to do. They live from their emotions. They are lighting their own fires.

> All intercessors have to be purified in God's fire before they can carry that fire to someone else.

Make no mistake: the brazen altar causes a death process, not a surgical process. God's fire needs to burn up your sin. So get rid of your strange fire of your own choosing, and let God replace it with the fire of purification.

All intercessors have to be purified in God's fire before they can carry that fire to someone else. You can't carry the fire to save someone else's life, and you can't successfully ask God to break the power of the enemy off that person until you have allowed God to burn the sin out of you.

Are you going through the fire? Good! That means you are on schedule.

Strange fires are lit by people who remain enslaved to their flesh while trying to serve the Lord.

The acts of the sinful nature are obvious: sexual immorality, impurity and debauchery; idolatry and witchcraft; hatred, discord, jealousy, fits of rage, selfish ambition, dissensions, factions and envy; drunkenness, orgies, and the like. I warn you, as I did before, that those who live like this will not inherit the kingdom of God.

—GALATIANS 5:19–21, NIV

Don't Jump Off the Altar

Not one of us has *made* it, no matter who we are or how long we have been saved. Yet God's grace (as symbolized by the number five, the width of the altar) and His will (as represented by the number three, the height of the altar) will carry each of us through to the other side of sacrifice.

Stay on the brazen altar until God Himself takes you off it. Then you will be prepared to move to the next level of prayer in His strength and power. But beware—you will be returned to the brazen altar *daily*.

> Don't jump off the altar while your sins and limitations are still being consumed.

Don't jump off the altar while your sins and limitations are still being consumed. If you jump off the altar too soon, you will be in danger. Not only could you fall back into sin, but the fire could go out. If you don't keep yourself on the altar like fresh wood that is laid upon it daily, the fire will go out. Your submitted life keeps the holy altar fire burning.

You can't rush this process. If you fall, get up and start again.

In God's perfect time, it will be all right to rise from the altar and head toward the holy place.

Stay on the brazen altar until God Himself takes you off it.

There hath no temptation taken you but such as is common to man: but God is faithful, who will not suffer you to be tempted above that ye are able; but will with the temptation also make a way to escape, that ye may be able to bear it.

—1 Corinthians 10:13, kjv

Section 5
THE FOUNDATIONAL GARMENT

Holy Clothing

When God gave instructions to Moses for the building of the tabernacle, He also gave very specific directions for the garments that Aaron and his sons were to wear as they performed their duties as priests in the tabernacle. Each priestly garment harmonized with the materials and colors that God instructed Moses to use in the holy place and in the East Gate. Like the tabernacle, these garments represent a spirit of excellence that God desires to manifest in the lives of every believer, especially those believers who have been called to prayer.

The Old Testament tabernacle was built according to God's specifications, and its priests were clothed exactly as God had ordained. In the same way, we who are the temple of the Holy Spirit must be built according to His specifications.

Are you in harmony with God? Is your life functioning according to God's pattern? If not, you will never see or experience His victorious glory. Each piece of your new spiritual prayer clothing has been custom-made according to God's measurements. You must be properly clothed spiritually for God to meet with you in prayer.

Your garments of righteousness work together with the God-ordained structure and the furniture (pattern) of the tabernacle to bring about successful results in prayer.

> *These garments represent a spirit of excellence that God desires to manifest in the lives of every believer, especially those believers who have been called to prayer.*

We who are the temple of the Holy Spirit must be built according to His specifications.

And it shall be our righteousness, if we observe to do all these commandments before the LORD our God, as he hath commanded us.

—DEUTERONOMY 6:25, KJV

RECEIVING YOUR PRIESTLY GARMENTS

*O*nly the obedient will be able to receive their priestly garments and ultimately enter the holy place in prayer. Anyone can come into the outer court through salvation, but many of those believers fail to honor God by being obedient. They fail to take off their old garments and step into their priestly ones.

The path of obedience requires that we enter the gate, wash at the laver, and sacrifice at the altar in obedience to God's pattern of prayer. That path of obedience allows us to pass from death into life, and it prepares us to be clothed for victory in intercessory prayer.

> The priestly garments represent everything we do after we enter the holy place.

The priestly garments represent everything we do after we enter the holy place. Whether it is worship or praise, preaching, baptizing, counseling—whatever we do—it must match up with Jesus Christ. If our works don't match Him, God won't show up, and the people will lose His blessings.

Many times the enemy binds us up in prayer (instead of us binding him), because we are improperly dressed. To keep that from happening, it is critical that you wear the right spiritual clothing—the clothing of righteousness.

Only the obedient will be able to receive their priestly garments and ultimately to enter the holy place in prayer.

He [Moses] put on Aaron the long undertunic, girded him with the long sash, clothed him with the robe, put the ephod (an upper vestment) upon him, and girded him with the skillfully woven cords attached to the ephod, binding it to him. And Moses put upon Aaron the breastplate; also he put in the breastplate the Urim and the Thummim [articles upon which the high priest put his hand when seeking the divine will concerning the nation]. And he put the turban or miter on his head; on it, in front, Moses put the shining gold plate, the holy diadem, as the Lord commanded him.

—LEVITICUS 8:7−9

Your Tunic of Righteousness

The foundational garment is the tunic of righteousness, which represents the righteousness of God. By wearing it underneath everything else, the other garments can fulfill their purposes.

All of Moses's priests wore white tunics, and the high priest wore additional garments over his tunic. The tunics allowed the priests to come safely before the awesome presence of God in the holy place.

God wants each one of us to put on our tunic of righteousness as the foundational garment for everything we do in prayer. So that we can be prepared to take up the burden of the Lord, our nakedness must be covered with a suitable garment, a special one that will permit us to enter the holy place and not perish.

> God wants you to live in righteousness 24/7, maintaining your tunic of righteousness in its Sunday condition.

You cannot come to church on Sunday and then go right back to living in sin until next Sunday. If you do, each time you enter the church you bring iniquity, bad attitudes, and deception, like so many other people in the church who are always up and down, in and out of fellowship. How can you expect God to keep cleaning you up?

You need to learn how God wants you to live—with His help at all times. He wants you to live in righteousness 24/7, maintaining your tunic of righteousness in its Sunday condition. The apostle Paul wrote, "I warn everyone among you not to estimate and think of himself more highly than he ought [not to have an exaggerated opinion of his own importance], but to rate his ability with sober judgment, each according to the degree of faith apportioned by God to him" (Rom. 12:3).

The foundational garment is the tunic of righteousness, which represents the righteousness of God.

Then the priests and Levites arose and blessed the people; and their voice was heard and their prayer came up to [God's] holy habitation in heaven.

—2 Chronicles 30:27

Your Spiritual Assignment

When God calls you into service, He gives you a level of faith that matches your spiritual assignment. When He speaks to you from the third realm and puts you in your assigned place, you will stay covered by His righteousness if you continue to function at that level of service.

Too many believers aspire to be high priests without having the faith to operate on that level. You must learn to be content and productive for God right where you are.

God doesn't need anything from your five fleshly senses: what you can see, smell, taste, hear, or touch. He doesn't want you to pay attention to your earthly senses when you are praying because they won't give you the spiritual information you need. While you're praying for someone's healing, your senses will inform you that the person is still sick. However, if you are wearing the pure white covering of faith-filled righteousness, you will be blind to your limited earthly understanding and able to pray according to God's pattern.

> Maintaining the righteousness of God in your life will initially be your biggest struggle in prayer.

It is vital that you learn to embrace the righteousness of God. Your spiritual white linen underclothing covers your human nature with the unassailable purity of God. You will need to learn to stop relying on your own human strength and to start leaning on His. Maintaining the righteousness of God in your life will initially be your biggest struggle in prayer.

It is the white tunic of righteousness that will help you to walk the path of obedience after you have washed at the brazen laver and sacrificed at the brazen altar. "So guard yourself in your spirit, and do not break faith" (Mal. 2:16, NIV).

When God calls you into service, He gives you a level of faith that matches your spiritual assignment and He keeps you covered by His righteousness.

For therein [in the gospel of Christ] is the righteousness of God revealed from faith to faith: as it is written, The just shall live by faith.

—Romans 1:17, KJV

Divine Nature Covers Old Nature

*C*hrist's divine nature covers your old nature. It is as you walk in obedience to God that He empowers you to "add to your faith virtue; and to virtue knowledge; and to knowledge temperance; and to temperance patience; and to patience godliness; and to godliness brotherly kindness; and to brotherly kindness charity" (2 Pet. 1:5–7, KJV).

If all these things remain in you, your prayer life will be fruitful. If you maintain your inner tabernacle, you will always come out of your prayer closet in victory. But if you fail to stay behind the covering of God's righteousness (by walking in disobedience after you have already been cleansed from sin at the brazen laver and the brazen altar), you will be spiritually blind. You will lack the divine nature of God. As a result, you will not be permitted into the holy place or the most holy place.

> If you fail to stay behind the covering of God's righteousness, you will be spiritually blind. You will lack the divine nature of God.

You can't serve a divine God from your lower nature. There's no match in the Spirit; light will not fellowship with darkness. This means that when you pray, God will not show up. You see, you cannot minimize the value of your white garments.

If you maintain your inner tabernacle, if you "give diligence to make your calling and election sure…if ye do these things, ye shall never fall" (2 Pet. 1:10, KJV). For when you are clothed in your white linen garments, you will be permitted to enter the second and third dimensions of prayer, which occur inside the tabernacle. Your victory is assured.

When you are clothed in your white linen garments, you will be permitted to enter the second and third dimensions of prayer, which occur inside the tabernacle. Your victory is assured.

[Jesus] hath given unto us all things that pertain unto life and godliness, through the knowledge of him that hath called us to glory and virtue: Whereby are given unto us exceeding great and precious promises: that by these ye might be partakers of the divine nature, having escaped the corruption that is in the world through lust.

—2 Peter 1:3–4, KJV

Are You Being Called to Higher Ground?

*I*n learning about the priestly garments, God wants us to discern the difference between a person who merely prays and one who understands that he or she has been called to intercession. I believe that every Christian is called to prayer, but there comes a season in our lives when we mature and are called to higher ground.

You must realize that once you allow God to mature you in character and to place a mantle of prayer upon your shoulders, you cannot choose to go back to being a spiritual baby when you hit a bump in the road. Things don't work that way in God's kingdom. It would be better never to touch God's mantle or to come into the knowledge of the power of righteousness than to turn and look back. You are responsible for everything you hear from God, whether you obey it or not, and you will be judged by God for what you do with what you hear from Him during your lifetime.

When you first came into the knowledge of Jesus Christ, you automatically became an enemy of Satan. He won't stop being your enemy, even if you decide to remain a spiritual baby. Because you have become an enemy of Satan, *you must receive your spiritual clothing, take up your weapons, and fight.* It's crazy to have inherited an enemy and not learn how to fight him. (And yet too many Christians live defeated lives because of this.)

Don't just talk about what the devil is doing to you—fight back.

> You cannot choose to go back to being a spiritual baby when you hit a bump in the road.

Because you have become an enemy of Satan, you must receive your spiritual clothing, take up your weapons, and fight.

Behold! I have given you authority and power to trample upon serpents and scorpions, and [physical and mental strength and ability] over all the power that the enemy [possesses]; and nothing shall in any way harm you.

—Luke 10:19

GET DRESSED TO COME INTO HIS PRESENCE

*N*ow that you have come through the outer court level, where anyone can enter—the lame, the broke, the busted, the disgusted—a new life of prayer is ready to open before your eyes.

No longer do you have to be like the people who have stayed behind in the outer court, always needing to be washed and rewashed for the same sins that God dealt with when they first came into the kingdom.

No longer do you have to be like the people who advance to the next level of prayer in the holy place, but they only stay because they are entertained by the light and the bread. (They never go beyond receiving somebody else's teachings about having a supernatural, face-to-face relationship with God, and they always need someone else to pray for them—they never graduate to praying for others.)

Until you have a real experience of the presence of the Lord, you can't claim to have a relationship with Him that will keep you on the right path. But once you have an experience where you are shaken to the core by His awesomeness, you want to stay where He is. You want to be righteous, and the infant spirit breaks off you.

Now, when you come to the house of the Lord, you can *bring* fire instead of merely coming again to *get* it. You don't have to linger in the outer court. You can be properly dressed, and you can go further in the things of God.

> Once you have an experience where you are shaken to the core by His awesomeness, you want to stay where He is. You want to be righteous, and the infant spirit breaks off you.

You don't have to linger in the outer court. You can be properly dressed and you can go further in the things of God.

Therefore if any person is [ingrafted] in Christ (the Messiah) he is a new creation (a new creature altogether); the old [previous moral and spiritual condition] has passed away. Behold, the fresh and new has come!

—2 CORINTHIANS 5:17

JESUS CHRIST IS YOUR RIGHTEOUSNESS

Every day I ask Him, "What do You want me to do, God? What do You want me to say? Where do You want me to go?" I can be on my way to the store when the power of God hits me, and I can end up laying my hands on someone and seeing that person be delivered. I don't have to work it up, because I'm not the one doing the work. Jesus Christ is living vicariously through me.

You too can go into the most holy place, because Christ lives vicariously through you. You don't have to go through the high priest. You can stand before the throne of God knowing that you are seated with Christ at the right hand of the Father—assuming you are keeping covered with the pure garments of righteousness.

> Cleanliness is a requirement for intercessors. Jesus Christ is your righteousness.

If you don't keep pure, the devil will notice, and he will give you a good old-fashioned whipping. You can't fake it, even if you appear to be religious. Remember the lesson of the seven sons of Sceva (Acts 19:13–16). Sceva was the chief of the priests, but his sons weren't qualified to cast out a demon. They paid for their presumption.

Cleanliness is a requirement for intercessors. When you put on your tunic of righteousness, that's your declaration. Jesus Christ is your righteousness. Now when you walk into the most holy place to battle in the Spirit, the devil will look at you and say, "Here comes Jesus."

You too can go into the most holy place, because Christ lives vicariously through you.

I will greatly rejoice in the Lord, my soul will exult in my God; for He has clothed me with the garments of salvation, He has covered me with the robe of righteousness, as a bridegroom decks himself with a garland, and as a bride adorns herself with her jewels.

—ISAIAH 61:10

RIGHTEOUS PRAYERS AVAILETH MUCH

*I*f you give up your righteousness, you give up your future. You won't be able to rebuke the devil out of a closet. You may have a gift, a talent, or a great ministry, but the righteousness of God is the only thing that demons will respect in a human being.

Tongues are not new to the devil, so your prayer language, knowledge of Scripture, worship, dancing, and shouting do not scare him. What really frightens him is looking at you—and being blinded by your righteousness.

> The righteousness of God is the only thing that demons will respect in a human being.

The light that comes from the secret place is unbearable to the enemy. So when you go into prayer dressed in your tunic of righteousness, the devil has to feel around for you because he can't open his eyes and see—the light is too bright.

Some people are satisfied with going to a building to worship God, but I want to dwell on His "holy hill" permanently. (See Psalm 15:1–5.) That means I'm letting God cover me in His righteousness and build a solid tabernacle in my spirit.

If you are letting God clothe you in His righteousness, you too can dwell permanently on His holy hill. You will be one who lives uprightly and blamelessly and who rejoices in doing things right. The devil can come, but he can't shake you. Temptation may rise, but it won't move you. Tribulation my come your way, but it's not going to defeat you. Your destiny is on the hill.

If you are letting God clothe you in His righteousness, you too can dwell permanently on His holy hill.

The effectual fervent prayer of a righteous man availeth much.

—JAMES 5:16, KJV

Section 6
THE GARMENTS OF COMPLETION

THE PRIESTLY WARDROBE

God is a God of meticulous detail. By giving precise, specific instructions for the making of the tabernacle and the priestly garments, the Old Testament helps us to understand what we can still do today to get into God's divine presence in the most holy place.

Because the tabernacle could not operate without the priests, the Lord saw fit to have the Old Testament priests dress a certain way. Every item of clothing was associated with an element used in constructing the temple. Today, the same truth applies to the church. It is not enough for a believer simply to attend church. As God's people, believers must *become* the church.

> Once we have accepted Jesus as our personal Savior, there must be a priesthood inside our earthly temple.

Once we have accepted Jesus as our personal Savior, there must be a priesthood inside our earthly temple. If there is no priesthood functioning within us, we become people who attend church but have no righteousness. We have come through the gate and accepted the works of Christ. We have repented of our sins and been washed by God's Word at the brazen laver. We have presented our bodies as living sacrifices at the brazen altar. Now we are clothed with the robe of righteousness, which is the first garment we receive when we are adopted into the royal priesthood.

Where do we go from here? If you intend to enter into the holy place, you must wear all of the garments of the priesthood.

If you intend to enter into the holy place, you must wear all of the garments of the priesthood.

You yourselves are full of goodness, complete in knowledge and competent to instruct one another. I have written you quite boldly on some points, as if to remind you of them again, because of the grace God gave me to be a minister of Christ Jesus to the Gentiles with the priestly duty of proclaiming the gospel of God.

—ROMANS 15:14–16, NIV

The Devil Cannot Follow You

God is trying to bring you all the way through the outer court where you live and pray according to human customs, traditions, and denominationalism. He's leading you into the realm of the Spirit, where the devil cannot follow you!

The deeper you go in God, the fainter the enemy's voice becomes. In the outer court, the enemy's voice has been loud in your ear, but the more you obey God and activate your garments, the more you will hear from God and the more distant the voice of Satan will become.

Going to another level of purification ordains you as an authentic intercessor. It equips you to travel into the Spirit realm, where the enemy can't follow. When you go into intercession, the only weapon the devil should possess against you is your past—and he will never win the battle when he tries to play the "past" game with you, because you will remind him of *his* past. ("You were thrown down from heaven, and Jesus stripped you of your authority. He even took the keys of death, hell, and the grave away from you.")

> Going to another level of purification equips you to travel into the Spirit realm, where the enemy can't follow.

God is leading you into the realm of the Spirit, where the devil cannot follow you!

Who shall ascend into the hill of the LORD? or who shall stand in his holy place? He that hath clean hands, and a pure heart.

—PSALM 24:3–4, KJV

THE SASH (BELT OF TRUTH)

After clothing Aaron with the tunic (robe of righteousness), Moses girded him with the sash. There were two belts in the priestly garments. The first belt went over the tunic, and the second belt was part of the ephod.

When you put on the garments of intercession, the belt of truth goes on top of the tunic of righteousness. Unlike the belt of the ephod, it is not visible to the naked eye. The belt of truth girds your loins. It holds your tunic together underneath the robe of blue, the ephod, and the breastplate. In order to walk in righteousness, you must embrace truth and keep it girded about you.

This belt symbolizes *readiness*—when you have it fastened, you are a servant who is always ready to go out into the world. This truth has two purposes: it makes you ready to work for God in prayer, and it is constantly working in you and for you.

When you go into intercession with your belt of truth in place, you simply speak the truth in prayer, which can only be done by speaking the Word of God. You have girded up the loins of your mind, and you can stand in a hard place for long periods of time without growing weary.

> The belt of truth girds your loins. In order to walk in righteousness, you must embrace truth and keep it girded about you.

You have girded up the loins of your mind, and you can stand in a hard place for long periods of time without growing weary.

Study to shew thyself approved unto God, a workman that needeth not to be ashamed, rightly dividing the word of truth.

—2 TIMOTHY 2:15, KJV

THE ROBE OF BLUE

*N*ext, Moses placed on Aaron the blue robe. (See Leviticus 8:7.) Blue represents *covering authority*. It also represents *divinity* and *grace*. These illustrate how you must go into prayer with a firm hold on your salvation.

The blue robe is for those who have matured spiritually. They are able to say, "I'm saved. I'm not trying to find a sneaky way out of righteousness, and I'm not trying to straddle the fence."

Intercessors are finished with sin. This doesn't mean that you will never make a mistake. But if you do, it will be because the devil caught you off guard. You will know that every time you sin deliberately, you lose ground. You will know that you cannot get your job done as an intercessor until you have whipped every demon in your own life.

> Blue represents *covering authority*. It also represents *divinity* and *grace*.

An intercessor who wears the robe of Christ's righteous divinity will *pray through* instead of merely *praying about*. When you are praying *about* something, you are still waiting for God to do it. When you are praying *through* something, you believe it was already done when you first declared the Word in prayer. There's a huge difference between going *to* a door and going *through* it.

Intercessors are finished with sin.

Make the robe [to be worn beneath] the ephod all of blue. There shall be a hole in the center of it [to slip over the head], with a binding of woven work around the hole…that it may not fray or tear.…Aaron shall wear the robe when he ministers, and its sound [*of bells on the skirt*] shall be heard when he goes…into the Holy of Holies before the Lord and when he comes out, lest he die there.

—EXODUS 28:31–32, 35

A Double Portion of Protection

Notice that the neckband of the priestly robe Moses gave to Aaron was reinforced. An extra band was woven around the neck opening to keep it from fraying or tearing. This symbolizes how your robe of authority is designed so it cannot be torn from you.

Your blue robe of authority is equated with the strength of your relationship with God in prayer. Righteousness is your passageway, the belt of truth enables you to stand firm, and your robe of authority makes it possible for you to resist the enemy effectively.

> Righteousness is your passageway, the belt of truth enables you to stand firm, and your robe of authority makes it possible for you to resist the enemy effectively.

You will be able to praise God with authority: "God, I praise You because You're *Jehovah Jireh,* my provider. I thank You because You are my righteousness." You praise Him because you know who He is.

Don't waste time praying until you can believe God will do something. You have to come to the throne of grace boldly—not wondering timidly if God is going to perform His Word. Don't waste time wondering if God will do what He said. Come expecting Him to tell you what to do next. When the devil tries to manipulate you with fear and intimidation, don't listen. Keep standing in prayer according to the will of God, knowing that the Spirit will reveal what you need to do.

Don't reject the robe of authority. Don't try to take the easy way out. God has allowed you to be placed in a deadlocked situation so that He can step into it through your prayers. As a priestly intercessor, your job is not to worry; your job is to keep the presence of the Lord in the room.

Don't reject the robe of authority. Don't try to take the easy way out.

Therefore, since we have a great high priest who has gone through the heavens, Jesus the Son of God, let us hold firmly to the faith we profess....Let us then approach the throne of grace with confidence, so that we may receive mercy and find grace to help us in our time of need.

—Hebrews 4:14, 16, niv

The Ephod

*A*fter receiving a robe of blue, the next garment Aaron received was the ephod, the upper vestment. The ephod was linen woven from multicolored threads: gold (representing *deity*), blue/turquoise (*divinity*), purple (*royalty*), scarlet (*servanthood* and *humanity*), and white (*purity*). It was girded onto the wearer with a belt, and the whole garment was worn on top, where everyone could see it.

Christ's ephod helps you to serve others by His grace, to help those who are weak come to maturity. It represents the mediator Jesus Christ, who was the perfect servant. When He clothes you in the ephod, it confirms the trials and tests you have overcome in order to get to this level. The gold threads show that you have already been through the testing of fire and that you're ready for more testing in prayer.

> Christ's ephod helps you to serve others by His grace, to help those who are weak come to maturity.

The ephod carried two onyx stones on its shoulders, and these stones were inscribed with the names of the twelve tribes of Israel in the order of their birthright. These same names were also inscribed on the breastplate, but in a different order. On the breastplate, they were ordered according to the will of God.

When you put on your ephod in prayer, you can be confident that God is able to do "exceeding abundantly above all that we ask or think" (Eph. 3:20, KJV), not according to the worldly order, but rather according to His declared will and His power.

The ephod confirms the trials and tests you have overcome in order to get to this level.

He put on Aaron the long undertunic, girded him with the long sash, clothed him with the robe, put the ephod (an upper vestment) upon him, and girded him with the skillfully woven cords attached to the ephod, binding it to him.

—Leviticus 8:7

THE BREASTPLATE

The breastplate was the next piece of clothing Aaron received. This garment is vital for an intercessor. On its surface were mounted twelve precious stones, representing the twelve tribes. (See Exodus 28:16–21.) Inside the breastplate was a slip of parchment containing the divine name of God, represented by the Urim and Thummim. (See Exodus 28:28–30.) *Urim* means "light," and *Thummim* means "completeness."

> God supernaturally binds people to your chest so that their burdens stay close to your heart.

The twelve precious stones represent the people you carry to God in prayer. The breastplate is worn upon the chest, indicating that the high priest carried the people's burdens close to his heart as he served in the tabernacle.

God supernaturally binds people to your chest so that their burdens stay close to your heart. As you pray, light enters the situation, and God starts perfecting to completion the thing for which you are praying. This is yet another way you know when He has truly girded you for intercession. Can you carry a name to the point of victory?

As you pray, light enters the situation, and God starts perfecting the thing to completion.

And Moses put upon Aaron the breastplate; also he put in the breastplate the Urim and the Thummim [articles upon which the high priest put his hand when seeking the divine will concerning the nation].

—LEVITICUS 8:8

THE MITER

*N*ow we will look at the miter, which is the headpiece, the final piece of the priestly garments. The miter was a turban, like a hat, with the distinguishing feature of a golden plate tied to the front. The inscription on the plate read, "HOLY TO THE LORD" (Exod. 28:36). This indicated that the nation of Israel was completely devoted to God and His service. It also reminded the priests never to take holiness for granted as they carried out their duties. At all times they were to conduct their lives in a way that was worthy of His name.

The miter can be likened to the helmet of salvation, a vital part of the spiritual armor that is required to wage war in prayer. "Take the helmet of salvation…praying always with all supplication in the Spirit, and watching thereunto with all perseverance and supplication for all saints" (Eph. 6:17–18, KJV).

The miter helps you watch and pray. God places it on your head after He has put everything else on you. He wants to remind you to pray without ceasing and to live in a way that is worthy of your calling.

> The miter can be likened to the helmet of salvation, a vital part of the spiritual armor that is required to wage war in prayer.

The miter helps you watch and pray. God wants to remind you to pray without ceasing and to live in a way that is worthy of your calling.

And he put the turban or miter on his head; on it, in front, Moses put the shining gold plate, the holy diadem, as the Lord commanded him.

—LEVITICUS 8:9

WHY DON'T YOU HAVE THE VICTORY?

Many of God's people do not have victory in their prayers. Why? Lack of power in prayer can always be traced to *discouragement* and *weariness*, and those characteristics take up residence in you when you fail to renounce sin.

You have to renounce any deception in your life if you expect to succeed in prayer. It's not enough to say, "His strength is made perfect in my weakness" or "God loves me." You need to remember what He tells us in Revelation 3:19: "Those whom I [dearly and tenderly] love, I tell their faults and convict and convince and reprove and chasten [I discipline and instruct them]. So be enthusiastic and in earnest and burning with zeal and repent [changing your mind and attitude]." Jesus is loving you when He rebukes and convicts you of sin. He is loving you when He tells you about your faults.

> Lack of power in prayer can always be traced to *discouragement* and *weariness,* and those characteristics take up residence in you when you fail to renounce sin.

The real proof that God loves you isn't the fact that you can feel goose bumps during a service. It's not because you are weeping. God demonstrates His love when He exposes your wrongdoings.

God identifies the reasons why you have fear instead of faith. He purifies you so your prayers won't be hindered. Now you will love Him as you never have before.

God identifies the reasons why you have fear instead of faith. He purifies you so your prayers won't be hindered.

Since through God's mercy we have this ministry, we do not lose heart. Rather, we have renounced secret and shameful ways; we do not use deception, nor do we distort the word of God. On the contrary, by setting forth the truth plainly we commend ourselves to every man's conscience in the sight of God.

—2 CORINTHIANS 4:1–2, NIV

You Are a Living Tabernacle

When you are fully clothed, you have been equipped to stand firmly as a royal priest before God. Having been summoned to serve others in prayer and clothed with the garments of preparation, you are ready to be anointed for your assignment and to enter the holy place.

In order to move into the realm of that which is holy, there must be a match—a coming together with God in agreement. He is the light of the world, and you bear His light as you bear the burden of prayer. Now everyone should be able to see the new you, even the enemy.

Be careful. If your life doesn't match your priestly clothing, then the anointing to be an intercessor won't be upon you. If there's no harmony between the colors of your garments and the life characteristics they represent, you won't experience the proper flow of the Spirit in prayer, and you won't see results.

Make your calling and election sure today, because you are the temple of the Holy Spirit, a living, breathing tabernacle, and you can have entry into His divine presence as you give Him entry into every situation that is brought before you.

In your spirit man, you can approach God right now.

> In order to move into the realm of that which is holy, there must be a match—a coming together with God in agreement.

Having been summoned to serve others in prayer and clothed with the garments of preparation, you are ready to be anointed for your assignment and to enter the holy place.

A time will come…indeed it is already here, when the true (genuine) worshipers will worship the Father in spirit and in truth (reality); for the Father is seeking just such people as these as His worshipers. God is a Spirit (a spiritual Being) and those who worship Him must worship Him in spirit and in truth (reality).

—JOHN 4:23–24

Section 7

THE TABERNACLE DOOR

Put on Jesus Christ

When people saw Aaron and his sons serving daily in the tabernacle, they knew by their special garments that they were operating in the authority of God—just as we operate in the authority of Christ, who is the ultimate High Priest.

The Old Testament priests put on the tunic, the trousers, the sash, the robe, the ephod, the breastplate, and the turban. In the same way, you "put on" Jesus Christ. You wear the attire of consecration, and you serve in the holy place. You don't have to perform feats of self-sacrifice to consecrate yourself, because you should be walking in the power of consecration every day.

> The only requirement to pray and see somebody be healed of cancer is that you must possess the High Priest deep in your spirit.

You don't have to be a bishop or an evangelist to pray and see somebody be healed of cancer. The only requirement is that you must possess the High Priest deep in your spirit. When you guard all that your priestly garments represent, you can rebuke the devil and walk in the *right now* power of God.

Staying properly clothed is a decision that must be made through the Word of truth, and not by your emotions. We can't trust our emotions (feelings), because the devil is a lying wonder. Don't listen to him.

Robed in righteousness and girded with truth, you will know God's power to save, heal, and deliver.

When you guard all that your priestly garments represent, you can rebuke the devil and walk in the right now *power of God.*

For ye are all the children of God by faith in Christ Jesus. For as many of you as have been baptized into Christ have put on Christ.

—Galatians 3:26–27, KJV

GUARD YOUR GARMENTS

*N*ever forget that the foundation of every garment is the tunic of righteousness. A true intercessor must consistently display the righteousness of the Lord. If you have truly guarded your garments of righteousness, God's power and wisdom will operate through you when you pray, and you will reap a great harvest. (See James 3:17–18.)

Your job as an intercessor is to get unfeigned wisdom from above. When you are operating in this wisdom according to the righteousness of God, you can pray with peace. You can be confronted with a person who is dying from cancer and experience the peace of God, because you know that He is in charge and that even death could be a route to healing.

> A true intercessor must consistently display the righteousness of the Lord.

Your tunic of righteousness will deliver you from any form of self-righteousness. It will keep you depending upon the strength of the Lord. Self-righteous believers have been deceived into spirituality that is not based on personal deliverance. They think they have the victory, when in reality they haven't even had any battles.

As you walk toward the door of the holy place, you must walk in the strength of the Lord, knowing that if it were up to you, you would have failed every test in the outer court.

Your tunic of righteousness will deliver you from any form of self-righteousness. It will keep you depending upon the strength of the Lord.

For in the gospel a righteousness from God is revealed, a righteousness that is by faith from first to last, just as it is written: "The righteous will live by faith."

—ROMANS 1:17, NIV

The Real Power of Grace

Only through the grace of God are we able to walk in Christ's righteousness. Grace is the strength of the Lord; it is what gives us power to overcome the evil tendencies of our flesh. It is a never-ending gift of God.

Although no human being has ever been able to live righteously by following the Law, God's grace can make us victorious over sin. (See Romans 5:20.)

Sadly, many people say they know the Lord when they don't really know Him—they only know *of* Him. They may appear to be operating from the holy place as they teach Scripture. But their teaching is based on an elementary level that does not include a full understanding of God's grace. Their listeners don't learn to live in the strength of the Lord; they just feel comfortable.

> Many people say they know the Lord when they don't really know Him—they only know *of* Him.

As son and daughters of God, we should never feel comfortable living in habitual sin, thinking, *Whatever I do is OK, because the Lord is gracious and merciful.* These people put so much emphasis on mercy and grace that the righteousness of God cannot transform their lives.

Grace is the strength of the Lord, and it is a never-ending gift of God.

He gives us more and more grace (power of the Holy Spirit, to meet this evil tendency and all others fully). That is why He says, God sets Himself against the proud and haughty, but gives grace [continually] to the lowly (those who are humble enough to receive it).

—James 4:6

TRUE NEWNESS OF LIFE

*W*hen we "put on" the Lord Jesus Christ, we can *habitually* live in newness of life!

Christians have to stop saying, "I'm going to keep messing up, because God will keep forgiving me," and embrace the *grace* that says, "When sin comes knocking at my door, the power of God is going to elevate and ignite me from within. God has given me power to stand against this evil tendency."

Do you see it? Every time you are able to say *no* to the devil, you are operating in grace. To have grace means you have power with God through His righteousness. That's what will bring you boldly into the holy place.

> Every time you are able to say *no* to the devil, you are operating in grace.

The grace of God will help you to guard your priestly garments. When, by grace, you put on Jesus Christ, you put on your garments, which are like the armor of God. The enemy recognizes clothes. He knows what you're wearing—and he knows when you are trying to stand against him with nothing on at all.

Embrace the grace that says, "When sin comes knocking at my door, the power of God is going to elevate and ignite me from within. God has given me power to stand against this evil tendency."

Put on God's complete armor, that you may be able to resist and stand your ground on the evil day [of danger], and, having done all [the crisis demands], to stand [firmly in your place]. Stand therefore [hold your ground], having tightened the belt of truth around your loins and having put on the breastplate of integrity and of moral rectitude and right standing with God.

—EPHESIANS 6:13–14

Called to the Threshing Floor

As an intercessor, you can never stop praying. You might be driving on the highway, and you will have to pull over onto the shoulder to pray. When you are a real intercessor, the Holy Spirit can catch you up into the Spirit realm at any time of day or night. An intercessor doesn't just work a regular schedule. He or she often doesn't sleep through the night. An intercessor will say, "God, whatever You want me to do, wherever You want me to go, whatever You want me to say—I'm willing."

Jesus, the High Priest, leads you into intercession. Only He is qualified to bring you into the holy place before the throne of God. He keeps pulling you to the threshing floor, the floor of prayer, on behalf of others.

Every time I think I have prayed something through and I'm done, the High Priest pulls me into intercession again on behalf of someone else. It could be a family member or a friend. It could be personal needs. I could be called to pray for the president of the United States.

I need to be ready to pray all the time. That means I need to be fully clothed in the garments that will permit me to enter into the holy place. Jesus is fully dressed in His priestly garments, and I must remain in agreement with Him.

> Jesus, the High Priest, leads you into intercession, to the threshing floor, the floor of prayer, on behalf of others.

An intercessor will say, "God, whatever You want me to do, wherever You want me to go, whatever You want me to say—I'm willing."

So then, brethren, consecrated and set apart for God, who share in the heavenly calling, [thoughtfully and attentively] consider Jesus, the Apostle and High Priest whom we confessed [as ours when we embraced the Christian faith].

—Hebrews 3:1

MAKING A STAND

To be an intercessor means that you know how to *stand strong* as you pray.

The biblical story of Shadrach, Meshach, and Abednego gives us a perfect example of the power to stand. (See Daniel 3:19–27.) You will remember how the furnace was so hot that it incinerated the guards who threw the three righteous men into the fire. But Shadrach, Meshach, and Abednego were not harmed. In fact, a fourth figure could be seen in the flames with them—Jesus Himself.

When the devil thinks that he's creating a fire to destroy you, he's really orchestrating a victory on your behalf. All you have to do is *stand*, with Jesus' help.

When you are properly dressed for intercessory prayer, you will be able to stand in any situation. You may even be dangerous to your enemies—too hot to handle! When you're standing in the purity and power of God, clothed by the High Priest, nothing shall by any means hurt you.

> When you're standing in the purity and power of God, clothed by the High Priest, nothing shall by any means hurt you.

All you have to do is stand, *with Jesus' help.*

Hold fast what you have, so that no one may rob you and deprive you of your crown.

—REVELATION 3:11

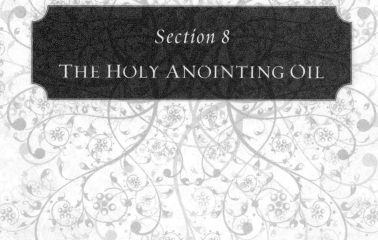

Section 8

THE HOLY ANOINTING OIL

Nothing But the Best

The Lord's anointing oil is necessary wherever the Lord sends you to pray for someone, whether it's to a hospital, a prison, a mental institution, or your own home.

As we have seen, God told Moses to take Aaron and his sons and clothe them. Then He told Moses to ordain them, sanctify them, and *anoint* them to serve as priests.

A special oil was created to anoint the priests. Today this oil represents the illumination of the Lord from His tabernacle in you. It is necessary wherever the Lord sends you to pray for someone, whether it's to a hospital, a prison, a mental institution, or your own home. As you submit yourself daily to being a living tabernacle of the Holy Spirit, every element in your tabernacle is anointed. You receive the anointing before you enter the holy place of prayer.

The Old Testament anointing oil was concocted by a master perfumer from the finest ingredients. No inferior imitation would do. The details of the composition of the oil that was used for anointing the priests was specified by God, just as He specifies the details of the requirements for a priestly intercessor.

Today we see too many imitations of the real anointing as Christians claim to have an anointing for anything they want to do. Scripture shows us that God has specific, high-quality ingredients that must be mixed together every time in order to become the true, sacred, supernatural anointing oil.

The details of the composition of the oil that was used for anointing the priests was specified by God, just as He specifies the details of the requirements for a priestly intercessor.

And you shall put them [the garments] on Aaron your brother and his sons with him, and shall anoint them and ordain and sanctify them [set them apart for God], that they may serve Me as priests.

—Exodus 28:41

Myrrh

To a quantity of pure olive oil, other ingredients were added. The first ingredient added to the holy anointing oil was 500 shekels of liquid myrrh. In Bible days, myrrh was a purifier. It was also used as an embalming fluid.

By specifying the use of myrrh, God is saying to us, "Not only do I have to purify your anointing, but I also have to embalm what I put to death so that when you see it again in the realm of the Spirit it won't affect you."

To God, it is of the utmost importance that His anointing is bestowed on believers who have matured beyond a childish desire for beauty and fame. We must want what He wants, and we must seek Him with a purified heart. We must settle it in our hearts that the old things have passed away and that everything is now covered with God's new life.

> In Bible days, myrrh was a purifier. It was also used as an embalming fluid.

God is saying to us, "Not only do I have to purify your anointing, but I also have to embalm what I put to death so that when you see it again in the realm of the Spirit it won't affect you."

And thou shalt anoint Aaron and his sons, and consecrate them, that they may minister unto me in the priest's office. And thou shalt speak unto the children of Israel, saying, This shall be an holy anointing oil unto me throughout your generations. Upon man's flesh shall it not be poured, neither shall ye make any other like it, after the composition of it: it is holy, and it shall be holy unto you.

—EXODUS 30:30–32, KJV

Sweet Cinnamon

The second ingredient that God specified for the anointing oil was 250 shekels of sweet cinnamon. This represents our attitude and how we treat other people.

> Sweet cinnamon represents our attitude and how we treat other people.

Christians who behave in a spiteful, mean way are missing an essential ingredient of the anointing. They haven't learned that when they are mistreated by others, they should bless the person even as they wrestle with the lies the person has told. In fact, they haven't learned that their actual anointing is likely to come by means of their enemies. The devil wants to hinder God's purpose for your life, but you can beat him at his own game.

As you learn to fight the devil instead of people, the spirit of the anointing can become so heavy around you that your enemies will be humbled by your brokenness. You can find the person who is your enemy and love that person into eternal life. As an intercessor, you must be equipped to take on the power and authority that you will need to fight on *behalf* of other people, not against them.

Ministry is for mature believers who have been washed, purified, sanctified, and broken under the anointing. Sweet cinnamon stands for your sweet attitude in response to your enemies.

Ministry is for mature believers who have been washed, purified, sanctified, and broken under the anointing.

When a man's ways please the Lord, He makes even his enemies to be at peace with him.

—Proverbs 16:7

SWEET CALAMUS

The third ingredient in the anointing oil was 250 shekels of sweet calamus. Calamus is also known as reed grass. It thrives on the banks of rivers and keeps on growing consistently, even when the plant gets old. In the life of an intercessor, it stands for the ever-growing maturity that is so important.

Unless you have all the ingredients of a true anointing— including the sweet calamus of mature stability in the Spirit— God will not be able to plant you in the midst of a mess that needs your prayers. You will need all that sweet calamus represents: patience, trust, flexibility, and increase of character.

If you aren't stabilized and mature in God, it's because you haven't allowed Him to lead you through the process of purification on your way to the threshing floor of prayer and intercession. When you miss a step in God, you become unstable in the anointing. If you don't have sweet calamus as part of your intercessory anointing, you will become stagnant in prayer, and you won't be able to go to deeper realms in the Spirit.

> In the life of an intercessor, sweet calamus stands for the ever-growing maturity that is so important.

You will need all that sweet calamus represents: patience, trust, flexibility, and increase of character.

Blessed is the man that walketh not in the counsel of the ungodly, nor standeth in the way of sinners, nor sitteth in the seat of the scornful. But his delight is in the law of the LORD; and in his law doth he meditate day and night. And he shall be like a tree planted by the rivers of water, that bringeth forth his fruit in his season; his leaf also shall not wither; and whatsoever he doeth shall prosper.

—PSALM 1:1–3, KJV

CASSIA

The final ingredient in the holy anointing oil was 500 shekels of cassia (a proportion equal to that of the myrrh). Cassia is fragrant and aromatic, and it is likely to have come from a plant that's related to cinnamon. Cassia had to be ground into a powder before being blended into the liquid oil with the other ingredients.

> Cassia stands for the way that you have been crushed as you have been prepared for ministry.

This spice represents the completion of your anointing. Cassia stands for the way that you have been crushed as you have been prepared for ministry. Your style of ministry, your personality, and your emotions have all been crushed in order to be blended into the sweet-smelling anointing of the divine presence.

When you get ready to move into intercession, this oil will anoint you, your Bible, and the place where you are kneeling down. No one can remove a true anointing from you, although you must maintain your garments in order to protect the anointing.

Finally, you are prepared to enter the holy place and approach the altar of incense, where true intercession is made.

No one can remove a true anointing from you, although you must maintain your garments in order to protect the anointing.

The Lord said to Moses, Take the best spices: of liquid myrrh 500 shekels, of sweet-scented cinnamon half as much, 250 shekels, of fragrant calamus 250 shekels, and of cassia 500 shekels...and of olive oil a hin. And you shall make of these a holy anointing oil, a perfume compounded after the art of the perfumer; it shall be a sacred anointing oil....And you shall anoint Aaron and his sons and sanctify (separate) them, that they may minister to Me as priests.

—EXODUS 30: 22–25, 30

EXPERIENCING HIS PRESENCE

Section 9

DIVINE PROTECTION

THE TABERNACLE COVERINGS

*E*ach piece of the furniture of the holy place relates to you in prayer. There are several tabernacle coverings (curtains), and each one is important to understand. They are closely related to the priestly garments.

The very idea of covering is important. When you are in the outer court (before you reach the maturity required to enter the holy place), you were exposed to whatever weather might blow your way. However, once you walk into the holy place, you are covered. The bad weather that the devil wants to send you cannot reach you.

> There are several tabernacle coverings (curtains), and they are closely related to the priestly garments.

Remember, the tabernacle consists of the holy place and the most holy place. God established the tabernacle so that there would be a place for His presence to *rest* among His people. Do you think the enemy could remain anywhere that God has chosen to rest? Absolutely not! As long as you remain properly attired, you can make intercession without the devil's interference.

The devil cannot follow you into the holy place. Just beware of falling back into outer court living. The only way he can come near you is if there is an opening in you, something you have not dealt with, such as fear, shame, offense, and so on.

Once you walk into the holy place, you are covered. The bad weather that the devil wants to send you cannot reach you.

Let them make Me a sanctuary, that I may dwell among them. And you shall make it according to all that I show you, the pattern of the tabernacle or dwelling and the pattern of all the furniture of it.

—Exodus 25:8–9

COVERING OF FINE-TWINED LINEN AND WOOL

xodus 26:1–14 lists the four (layered) tabernacle coverings. The first tabernacle curtain was woven of white "fine twined linen" and three different colors of wool: turquoise, purple, and scarlet, the same basic material that was used to weave the priestly ephod, although the ephod also had a gold strand woven in with the other colors.

As we learned when we read about the ephod, the white represents purity, turquoise represents divinity, purple represents royalty, and scarlet represents servanthood and humanity. The four colors woven together in the first tabernacle covering were embroidered with ornate figures of cherubim, a lion, an eagle, and an ox.

The fact that these colors of fine-twined linen and wool match those of the ephod shows us how our foundation as intercessors is the same as the foundational covering of God's resting place. God's truth is verified by two displays, just as He will not only perform His Word, but also be in the midst of it.

> The first tabernacle curtain was woven of white "fine twined linen" and three different colors of wool: turquoise, purple, and scarlet, the same basic material that was used to weave the priestly ephod.

The fact that these colors of fine-twined linen and wool match those of the ephod shows us how our foundation as intercessors is the same as the foundational covering of God's resting place.

If two of you on earth agree (harmonize together, make a symphony together) about whatever [anything and everything] they may ask, it will come to pass and be done for them by My Father in heaven. For wherever two or three are gathered (drawn together as My followers) in (into) My name, there I AM in the midst of them.

—MATTHEW 18:19–20

DIVINE IMAGES ON THE COVERING

The first covering of the tabernacle was embroidered with an intricate representation of the images of cherubim. These images have significance in prayer. What do they represent?

We are told in the Scriptures that the *cherubim* live around the throne of God, exalting Him continually and reflecting His glory. (They are not the same as angels, who work at God's behest in the service of human beings.)

On the first covering of the tabernacle, the intricate representation of the cherubim corresponds to the intricate workings of the Holy Spirit on behalf of the Father and the Son. As you pray, the cherubim remind you of the life, ministry, death, burial of the Lord Jesus Christ, and of His resurrection into glory.

When you walk into the holy place clothed in your priestly garments, a powerful divine match takes place. You are in divine agreement with the will of God, and you can walk with confident authority.

Satan has to respect your right to be there, However, if you try to go into intercession "illegally," with something about you that isn't entirely holy, the devil has a right to control your mind, to attack you, to take you out—because you are missing a part of the pattern.

※ ✝ ※

When you walk into the holy place clothed in your priestly garments, you are in divine agreement with the will of God and you can walk with confident authority.

※ ✝ ※

You shall make the tabernacle with ten curtains; of fine twined linen, and blue and purple and scarlet [stuff], with cherubim skillfully embroidered shall you make them.

—EXODUS 26:1

Covering of Goats' Hair

The second layer of covering over the tabernacle was woven from black goats' hair. This layer of the curtains, or the tent, was placed on top of the first layer. ("And make curtains of goats' hair to be a [second] covering over the tabernacle," Exod. 26:7.)

Under the Law, goats were used to atone for the sins of individuals, from rulers to common people. (See Leviticus 4:22–5:13.) Making curtains out of goats' hair reminds you of how you, as an intercessor who is covered within the tabernacle, receive the grace to carry the burden of the Lord for anyone, anywhere, at any time, without becoming offended or affected by the person's sin.

You are able to carry sins to God because Jesus was able to do it. He bore the sin of humankind so that believers could become the righteousness of God.

This covering of goats' hair was laid directly on top of the first covering, in the same way as God has covered your own sin completely. You can stand secure in this knowledge.

> This covering of goats' hair was laid directly on top of the first covering, in the same way as God has covered your own sin completely.

Goats' hair curtains remind you of how you receive the grace to carry the burden of the Lord for anyone, anywhere, at any time, without becoming offended or affected by the person's sin.

For our sake He made Christ [virtually] to be sin Who knew no sin, so that in and through Him we might become [endued with, viewed as being in, and examples of] the righteousness of God [what we ought to be, approved and acceptable and in right relationship with Him, by His goodness].

—2 Corinthians 5:21

COVERING OF RAMS' SKINS

*T*he third layer of the tabernacle covering was made from rams' skins dyed or tanned red. Rams were used in guilt offerings, and two rams were used in the sacrifices when Aaron and his sons were ordained into the priesthood.

The ram is a *sacrifice*, a *substitute*, a *provision*, and a *symbol of consecration* for priestly service. This makes the ram a powerful symbol as the third covering. You can consider how it relates to the three-in-one (Father, Son, and Holy Spirit).

Through this rams' skin covering, God speaks to you from Isaiah 1:18: "Come now, and let us reason together, says the Lord. Though your sins are like scarlet *[like the color of the ram's skin dyed red]*, they shall be as white as snow; though they are red like crimson, they shall be like wool."

Remember this when you are entering into intercession. Don't ever forget Christ's perfect work for you. Because of the sacrifice of His own blood, you will be able to stand faithfully for others.

> The ram is a *sacrifice*, a *substitute*, a *provision*, and a *symbol of consecration* for priestly service.

Because of the sacrifice of Christ's own blood, you will be able to stand faithfully for others.

Therefore He is able also to save to the uttermost (completely, perfectly, finally, and for all time and eternity) those who come to God through Him, since He is always living to make petition to God and intercede with Him and intervene for them. [Here is] the High Priest [perfectly adapted] to our needs, as was fitting—holy, blameless, unstained by sin, separated from sinners, and exalted higher than the heavens.

—HEBREWS 7:25–26

COVERING OF BADGERS' SKIN

The fourth and final tabernacle covering was made of badgers' skin (translated as dolphin or porpoise skin in the Amplified Bible). This layer was the final cover that provided overall protection for each of the other layers. These skins may also have been used to cover the tabernacle elements as the Israelites moved from one location to another.

These skins were strong. They could protect the other layers of protection. The tabernacle could be free from dirt, storms, and heat or cold. Nothing could penetrate the skins. No matter what the weather was like outside, the glory still remained on the inside.

> No matter what the weather was like outside, the glory still remained on the inside.

The same is true for you as you make intercession, clothed in your priestly garments and covered by the layers of God's provision—you will be protected against any outside onslaught of the devil. Even when you move from place to place, you are like the living temple of the Lord, protected and filled with His presence.

Even when you move from place to place, you are like the living temple of the Lord, protected and filled with His presence.

You shall make a [third] covering for the tent of rams' skins tanned red, and a [fourth] covering above that of dolphin or porpoise skins.

—EXODUS 26:14

Now Let Us Come Boldly

*I*t is interesting to note that while specific measurements were given for the first two coverings (curtains), there are no definite measurements for the second two, the rams' skin covering and the badgers' skin covering. This represents the fact that there is no measurement for Christ's divine substitution on our behalf. His divine protection against the wiles of Satan is also without measure.

The Lord God has given His Spirit to His Son Jesus without measure, and as long as we possess the Spirit of Christ, there is no limit to what we can do through prayer in Him.

We can come boldly to the throne of God, because the full price has already been paid; the work has already been done. You are fully covered and free to become a fellow intercessor with Jesus, the greatest intercessor of them all.

You are fully covered and free to become a fellow intercessor with Jesus, the greatest intercessor of them all.

Wait and listen, everyone who is thirsty! Come to the waters; and he who has no money, come, buy and eat! Yes, come, buy [priceless, spiritual] wine and milk without money and without price [simply for the self-surrender that accepts the blessing].

—ISAIAH 55:1

Section 10

THE HOLY PLACE

On the Threshing Floor

The priests entered the holy place for two reasons, and so do you.

First, they entered to perform the service of the Lord. They replaced the shewbread regularly; it represents the Word of God. They kept the menorah (lampstand) filled with olive oil and burning; this represents the light of the Lord and the oil of the anointing. They also kept a constant fire burning on the altar of incense (a place of worship and total surrender), which ensured that the glory of the Lord was maintained.

Second, they entered in order to lie prostrate before the Lord. They were wholly devoted to God, and they were separated from everyone else, even their fellow priests.

The holy place is your place of separation, and separation is at the heart of the threshing process. Therefore, the holy place is your threshing floor.

To thresh means to separate the seeds of grain from the straw. You entered into a personal threshing process as soon as you entered the gate to the outer court in prayer. Personal repentance separated you from sin so that you could be obedient to God. Now the separation process continues as you live within His purpose.

> The holy place is your place of separation, and separation is at the heart of the threshing process. Therefore, the holy place is your threshing floor.

You entered into a personal threshing process as soon as you entered the gate to the outer court in prayer. Now the separation process continues as you live within His purpose.

But you are a chosen race, a royal priesthood, a dedicated nation, [God's] own purchased, special people, that you may set forth the wonderful deeds and display the virtues and perfections of Him Who called you out of darkness into His marvelous light.

—1 Peter 2:9

The Table of Shewbread

When you enter the holy place, the table of shewbread is on your right. The table was built from acacia wood and overlaid with gold. This represents humanity (wood) covered by the deity of Jesus Christ (gold).

The shewbread, or bread of the presence of God, consisted of twelve loaves that were baked every Friday so they could replace the week-old loaves on the Sabbath (Saturday). The old loaves were still fresh enough to be divided among the priests. This corresponds with how the Word of God is our fresh bread daily.

In the New Testament, we see the people asking Jesus for bread. His response: "I am the Bread of Life. He who comes to Me will never be hungry, and he who believes in and cleaves to and trusts in and relies on Me will never thirst any more (at any time)" (John 6:35). Rest assured that when you pray, you commune with Christ and will lack nothing.

As an intercessor, you must eat of Christ; you have to digest the Word daily to maintain a transformed life. The bread will give you fresh strength daily, and the Word will turn into power on others' behalf. Come to the table and partake.

> As an intercessor, you have to digest the Word daily to maintain a transformed life.

The bread will give you fresh strength daily, and the Word will turn into power on others' behalf.

Make a table of acacia wood—two cubits long, a cubit wide and a cubit and a half high. Overlay it with pure gold and make a gold molding around it. Also make around it a rim a handbreadth wide and put a gold molding on the rim....Put the bread of the Presence on this table to be before me at all times.

—Exodus 25:23–25, 30, NIV

THE GOLDEN CANDLESTICK

The golden candlestick was the menorah, the seven-branched lamp that cast its light into the holy place. It symbolizes the light of illumination, divine understanding, insight, and revelation. For an intercessor, this means that you will be able to see and apply the Word in your prayer.

The menorah was molded from a talent of solid gold. The stem represents God and the six branches represent mankind (the church), which has been born out of Him.

According to Jewish tradition, Moses found it impossible to envision the menorah from God's verbal instructions, so God showed him one made of fire and then caused a golden menorah to be formed supernaturally. This suggests to us that when we enter the holy place of prayer, illumined by the menorah, we have come to the place where God begins to perform everything He reveals to us in prayer.

You receive the illumination, and God does the work!

When we enter the holy place of prayer, illumined by the menorah, we have come to the place where God begins to perform everything He reveals to us in prayer.

> You shall make a lampstand of pure gold. Of beaten and turned work shall the lampstand be made, both its base and its shaft; its cups, its knobs, and its flowers shall be of one piece with it. Six branches shall come out of the sides of it; three branches of the lampstand out of the one side and three branches out of its other side.
>
> —EXODUS 25:31–32

The menorah symbolizes the light of illumination, divine understanding, insight, and revelation.

Manifestation of the Supernatural

The intricate design of the golden menorah was a manifestation of the supernatural meaning of the lampstand. The word *manifest* means "readily perceived by the senses, easily understood by the mind." In the images that appeared on the golden lampstand, we have an obvious representation of kingdom truths.

The candlestick was decorated with almonds and flowers. Do you remember how Aaron's rod miraculously budded and blossomed with almonds? (See Numbers 17:8.) The almond speaks of everlasting resurrection, and the flower represents everlasting beauty.

Can people see divine beauty and sweetness in you? (Remember that by the time you get to the menorah, you have already received an anointing that includes the sweetness of cinnamon and calamus.)

When the holy lampstand was made, the gold was beaten and formed into almonds and blossoms, and it shone with reflected the light. In the same way, God wants each of us to manifest His truth to everyone we meet.

> The intricate design of the golden menorah was a manifestation of the supernatural meaning of the lampstand.

In the same way, God wants each of us to manifest His truth to everyone we meet.

Three cups made like almond blossoms, each with a knob and a flower on one branch, and three cups made like almond blossoms on the other branch with a knob and a flower; so for the six branches coming out of the lampstand; and on the [center shaft] itself you shall [make] four cups like almond blossoms with their knobs and their flowers.... Their knobs and their branches shall be of one piece with it; the whole of it one beaten work of pure gold.

—Exodus 25:33–34, 36

THE NECESSITY OF SACRIFICE

One final, powerful aspect of the golden candlestick is the fact that it was kept lit by the coals from the brazen altar. For us, this translates into a revelation about sacrifice. If there has never been any sacrifice in your life, and if you fail to willingly put yourself on the altar of sacrifice daily, then there will be no fire to light the golden candlestick in your life, and there will be no corresponding reflection of God's character for others to see.

To put it the other way around, if your sacrificial fire goes out, the illuminating flames on the golden candlestick will be extinguished. Personal sacrifice safeguards your character and assists your understanding of what God desires to do in the lives of the people for whom you are praying.

Lying next to the menorah on the threshing floor of prayer, you are separated unto the Lord, and your ears hear His voice. You can worship and intercede with a clear idea of God's will.

> If you fail to willingly put yourself on the altar of sacrifice daily, then there will be no fire to light the golden candlestick in your life, and there will be no corresponding reflection of God's character for others to see.

Personal sacrifice safeguards your character and assists your understanding of what God desires to do in the lives of the people for whom you are praying.

I will pray with my spirit [by the Holy Spirit that is within me], but I will also pray [intelligently] with my mind and understanding; I will sing with my spirit [by the Holy Spirit that is within me], but I will sing [intelligently] with my mind and understanding also.

—1 CORINTHIANS 14:15

KEEP THE PURE OIL BURNING

The flames on the golden lampstand were able to illuminate the holy place without going out because the lamp was filled with the pure oil of crushed olives. This symbolizes the pure anointing of the Holy Spirit.

The process of obtaining the pure olive oil is instructive; it reminds us of the process of separation on the threshing floor. The olives grow to maturity, and the fruit falls to the ground. Harvesters beat the trees with long sticks to yield the rest of the crop, and they gather all the olives together. Then, in biblical times, the oil was extracted by crushing the olives in the hollow of a stone or by treading upon them by foot.

> The lamp was filled with the pure oil of crushed olives. This symbolizes the pure anointing of the Holy Spirit.

The first collection of oil (what today we would term "extra virgin") was the purest. That was the oil that was used to keep the menorah burning.

In our lives, there is no anointing oil without a corresponding beating and crushing and pressing process. This shows us that the trials of our life can contribute directly to our anointing!

In our lives, there is no anointing oil without a corresponding beating and crushing and pressing process.

You shall command the Israelites to provide you with pure oil of crushed olives for the light, to cause it to burn continually [every night].

—EXODUS 27:20

TONGUES OF FIRE

To better relate the golden candlestick to your life as an intercessor, review the account of what happened on the Day of Pentecost, shortly after Jesus' ascension into heaven. (See Acts 2:1–4.)

Just as the golden menorah needed to be filled with fresh oil, so we believers need to be filled with the Spirit as the disciples were on the Day of Pentecost. If you are not truly filled with the Spirit, your fire cannot burn cleanly, and it cannot be sustained for long.

Be careful that people do not talk you into falsely manifesting the Holy Spirit. Take your time. Make sure that what you have is straight from God, not from someone's ideas of the baptism of the Spirit. Allow your filling to be evident before you start interceding for others. Without that infilling, there will be no supernatural utterance from heaven in your prayer closet.

Everything about the ministry God has given you must remain well lit with the fire that comes from God.

> Just as the golden menorah needed to be filled with fresh oil, so we believers need to be filled with the Spirit as the disciples were on the Day of Pentecost.

Without that infilling, there will be no supernatural utterance from heaven in your prayer closet.

When the day of Pentecost had fully come, they were all assembled together in one place, when suddenly…there appeared to them tongues resembling fire, which were separated and distributed and which settled on each one of them. And they were all filled (diffused throughout their souls) with the Holy Spirit and began to speak in other (different, foreign) languages (tongues), as the Spirit kept giving them clear and loud expression [in each tongue in appropriate words].

—ACTS 2:1–4

THE GOLDEN ALTAR OF INCENSE

The golden altar of incense is the third and central piece of furniture in the holy place. Like the table of shewbread, the altar was made of acacia wood and overlaid with gold. Here again, we see a representation of humanity overlaid with the deity of God, positioned in the middle of the holy place to show us that intercession is the heart of God.

The first altar, the brazen altar, was constructed of acacia wood overlaid with bronze. If we embrace only that altar of sacrifice, our prayers will have limitations similar to the impurities of bronze. We want to pray from the second altar, the altar of incense, because we want our prayers to manifest the divine purity that is represented by the pure gold.

The altar was three feet in height, which corresponded to the height of the ark of the covenant. In practice, this means that when you worship at the golden altar, it brings you to the right level, where you can commune with God according to His pattern.

> The altar of incense was made of acacia wood and overlaid with gold (humanity overlaid with deity), positioned in the middle of the holy place to show us that intercession is the heart of God.

The purpose of the golden altar was threefold: prayer, intercession, and worship. Having been initially kindled by God and rekindled continually by the coals of the altar of sacrifice, the fire on the altar of incense never went out.

The purpose of the golden altar was threefold: prayer, intercession, and worship.

And you shall make an altar to burn incense upon; of acacia wood you shall make it....And you shall overlay it with pure gold, its top and its sides round about and its horns....And Aaron shall burn on it incense of sweet spices; every morning when he trims and fills the lamps he shall burn it. And when Aaron lights the lamps in the evening, he shall burn it, a perpetual incense before the Lord throughout your generations.

—EXODUS 30:1, 3, 7–8

To Become an Intercessor

When you become an intercessor, you stand in the place of other people before God. You act as the point of contact to cause Satan to yield or surrender to the will of God. You grant or transfer authority according to God's will.

When you intercede, you stand in the gap for someone else, and you don't give up until the enemy has fully surrendered the territory he has occupied unlawfully.

Your prayers impinge and infringe upon the enemy; they strike and collide with the enemy. They surprise him, because they advance beyond the limits of the outer court, where you merely accept and acknowledge the situations you pray for. Your prayers advance all the way to the holy place, where Satan cannot contradict them and where they match up with the will of God.

When you are a true intercessor, you never stop praying. And God never stops responding to your prayers, because they are prayed from within His holy sanctuary.

> When you intercede, you stand in the gap for someone else, and you don't give up until the enemy has fully surrendered the territory he has occupied unlawfully.

A true intercessor never stops praying. And God never stops responding.

Thus saith the LORD, the Holy One of Israel, and his Maker, Ask me of things to come concerning my sons, and concerning the work of my hands command ye me.

—ISAIAH 45:11, KJV

Incense: Sweet, Pure, and Holy

*T*he holy incense that burned continually upon the coals of the golden altar was made up of several ingredients. The characteristics of the ingredients of the incense show us more about our prayers, worship, and intercession.

Stacte is a resin that oozes naturally from the storax tree. I believe this means that our prayers arise naturally and cannot be programmed. *Onycha* came from a shellfish that lived in the depths of the Red Sea. This means that you must have depth in your worship, and your prayers and songs cannot be rote repetition. *Galbanum* is a bitter resin that was acquired by splitting a tree branch. In the same way, we have bitter experiences and difficult seasons in our lives, and we must offer them up to God as we continue to pray. *Frankincense* was collected early in the morning from the Boswellia tree. Likewise, when we seek God early (meaning either morning or in a timely fashion), we will obtain what we need for our prayers.

> The characteristics of the ingredients of the incense show us more about our prayers, worship, and intercession.

To temper all these ingredients together, *salt* was used. Remember that you are the "salt of the earth" (Matt. 5:13)—especially as you function in your priestly role as an intercessor. You are the key element that brings it all together at the altar.

You are the "salt of the earth"—especially as you function in your priestly role as an intercessor. You are the key element that brings it all together at the altar.

Then the Lord said to Moses, Take sweet spices—stacte, onycha, and galbanum, sweet spices with pure frankincense, an equal amount of each—and make of them incense, a perfume after the perfumer's art, seasoned with salt and mixed, pure and sacred.

—Exodus 30:34–35

Section 11

THE POWER OF INTERCESSION

Entering the Most Holy Place

As you look straight ahead at the entrance through the veil, you will see the golden altar of incense. It is the nearest piece of furniture to God's divine presence behind the veil.

Anyone could come into the outer court and wash at the brazen laver before sacrificing at the brazen altar. But only the priests and the high priest were allowed to serve in the holy place where the altar was. And only the high priest could enter into the most holy place.

As you have learned, the sacred ingredients of the holy incense were carefully measured and blended before they were beaten into a fine powder, sprinkled on the coals, and burned to release a sweet fragrance.

When you are a true intercessor, anyone who comes into your presence should be able to feel the presence of God upon you. There should be a sweet odor of prayer and worship wherever you go.

> Anyone should be able to feel the presence of God upon a true intercessor.

There should be a sweet odor of prayer and worship wherever a true intercessor goes.

But thanks be to God, who always leads us in triumphal procession in Christ and through us spreads everywhere the fragrance of the knowledge of him. For we are to God the aroma of Christ among those who are being saved and those who are perishing. To the one we are the smell of death; to the other, the fragrance of life.

—2 Corinthians 2:14–16, NIV

The Trap of Pride and Arrogance

As we consider the meaning of the holy place today, we should note a potential problem: pride. As we learn when we read the story of King Uzziah (2 Chron. 26), it is possible to begin well and end badly.

King Uzziah began to trust in his own strength instead of in God's. In essence, he began to say, "I don't need the Lord anymore. I can handle this on my own." In an effort to serve as his own priest, King Uzziah passed the brazen laver and altar, and went straight into the holy place where he didn't belong.

> It doesn't matter how faithful you have been in the past, if you fail to be consistently faithful.

It can be the same with us. It doesn't matter how faithful you have been in the past, if you fail to be consistently faithful. You may say, "Every Sunday morning they ask me to lead in prayer because God has an anointing on my life." Be careful. Don't pass the brazen laver and altar without stopping and assume that you can enter the holy place. When you reach the holy place, you must be giving God your praise, worship, and all that you are—for His glory only.

Don't pass the brazen laver and altar without stopping and assume that you can enter the holy place.

After Uzziah became powerful, his pride led to his downfall. He was unfaithful to the LORD his God, and entered the temple of the LORD to burn incense on the altar of incense. Azariah the priest with eighty other courageous priests of the LORD followed him in. They confronted him and said, "It is not right for you, Uzziah, to burn incense to the LORD. That is for the priests, the descendants of Aaron, who have been consecrated to burn incense. Leave the sanctuary, for you have been unfaithful; and you will not be honored by the LORD God."

—2 Chronicles 26:16–18, NIV

PRESUMPTION IN THE PRIESTHOOD

*S*cripture warns us that it is a dangerous thing to elevate yourself to the office of priest before you have been purified. Remember the stories of Korah (Num. 16) and Aaron's sons Nadab and Abihu (Lev. 10).

God alone can call you to stand in the midst of the congregation and minister the Word of God (which is the shewbread) or to be a part of the moving of the Spirit (which is the candlestick). You must wait upon the Lord to be called to minister by way of intercession.

> You must wait upon the Lord to be called to minister by way of intercession.

Some believers create all kinds of things of their own design and mix them together, calling it "God." But continual sacrifice and brokenness are required to reach that depth of relationship and communication with God where God speaks to you face-to-face, directly and clearly. Though God desires for everybody to have this level of relationship, you have to lay yourself on the sacrificial altar and wait until He says you are qualified to be with Him in the holy place. Otherwise, the workings of your flesh will contaminate the sweet mixture of holy incense.

Continual sacrifice and brokenness are required to reach that depth of relationship and communication with God where God speaks to you face-to-face, directly and clearly.

There is a way which seems right to a man and appears straight before him, but at the end of it is the way of death.

—PROVERBS 14:12

There's Power in Following the Pattern

*D*o you understand and embrace the power of the golden altar of incense? Like Aaron, who learned from what happened to Korah and his own sons, you must learn to guard your garments and minister at the golden altar every morning and every night—because you must stand in the gap for those who need an answer from the Lord.

Remember, the high-priestly garments include the tunic and breeches (*righteousness*), the sash (*God's strength*), the blue robe (*authority*), and the ephod, which symbolized that the priest has been *proven* for his priestly role. They also include the breastplate with the Urim and Thummim (*light and completeness*) and the miter with crown, which symbolized *devotion* to the Lord.

If the divine pattern is followed, it is possible to enter the holy place, where nothing stands between the priest and his God. The same is true for you—if you follow God's pattern, *there is no veil* between Him and you.

When Jesus shed His blood on the cross, the temple veil was torn from top to bottom. Now any of us can stand before the most holy place as priests unto God, offering up the sweet, pure, and holy incense of our worship and intercession.

> Guard your garments and minister at the golden altar every morning and every night—because you must stand in the gap for those who need an answer from the Lord.

If you follow God's pattern, there is no veil between Him and you.

Now to Him Who, by (in consequence of) the [action of His] power that is at work within us, is able to [carry out His purpose and] do superabundantly, far over and above all that we [dare] ask or think [infinitely beyond our highest prayers, desires, thoughts, hopes, or dreams]—to Him be glory in the church and in Christ Jesus throughout all generations forever and ever.

—Ephesians 3:20–21

EVERYTHING THROUGH JESUS

*J*esus gave His life so that you could live and restore others to a right relationship with God. That's why you have to come through His completed works at every step of the pattern of prayer. You can do all things through Christ, but without Him you can do nothing.

As you prepare to go into the most holy place behind the veil, you know He's alive. When you lie at His feet in prayer and intercession, whether it's day, night, summer, spring, or winter, you know He's the only one who can keep you. In trials and tribulations, He is Lord. When the devil tries to wipe you out and tell you that you're not going to make it, Jesus is "exceeding abundantly" able to keep you alive and take you to your next level.

> You can do all things through Christ, but without Him you can do nothing.

You can have complete hope in Him. This hope is steadfast and sure, and it will anchor your soul (your mind, emotions, and will).

He's the only one who can keep you. In trials and tribulations, He is Lord.

[Now] we have this [hope] as a sure and steadfast anchor of the soul [it cannot slip and it cannot break down under whoever steps out upon it—a hope] that reaches farther and enters into [the very certainty of the Presence] within the veil, where Jesus has entered in for us [in advance], a Forerunner having become a High Priest forever.

—HEBREWS 6:19–20

Section 12

ETERNAL COMMUNION

THE ARK OF THE COVENANT

As with all the other elements of the tabernacle and its furniture, God gave specific instructions to Moses for the construction and contents of the ark of the covenant. We read about it in Exodus chapters 16 and 25 and Numbers chapter 17. The ark was overlaid with solid gold on the inside and outside, which represents *the perfected union of God and man.*

Three elements were housed in the ark: (1) the testimonial tablets (Exod. 24:12), which represent *the perfected Word* in your life; (2) Aaron's rod that budded (Num. 17:8–10), which is a *sign against rebellion to God-given authority*; and (3) an omer of manna, which represents *supernatural provision* (Exod. 16:32–34).

Because these three elements were maintained inside the ark, it housed the glory of God. Without them, the ark became just another empty gold box. We must understand that in order for us to walk in the perfected power of God, these same elements must be housed in the ark of our hearts:

(1) The Word must be manifest in our everyday lives; (2) obedience, not rebellion, must characterize our lives; and (3) we must trust God, not man, for everything we need.

> Because these three elements were maintained inside the ark, it housed the glory of God.

The Word must be manifest in our everyday lives; obedience, not rebellion, must characterize our lives; and we must trust God, not man, for everything we need.

They shall make an ark of acacia wood: two and a half cubits long, a cubit and a half wide, and a cubit and a half high. You shall overlay the ark with pure gold, inside and out, and make a gold crown, a rim or border, around its top....And you shall put inside the ark the Testimony [the Ten Commandments] which I will give you.

—EXODUS 25:10–11, 16

THE ARK OF YOUR HEART

I believe that the ark represents the human heart, the deepest, most intimate part of who you are, and the place where the glory of God can take up residence and transform everything around you.

Does your heart house these three elements? (Turn back a page to "The Ark of the Covenant.") If so, you will be able to dwell in the most holy place of God's glory, and your prayers will be answered. If you follow the steps of purification and death to self, you will have these elements within the ark of your heart. And if you continue to repeat the cleansing process, you will be able to maintain them there.

It's as if the floor of the holy place is a threshing floor, where you have been separated unto His presence (and parted from your personal and worldly issues). This is far more than obtaining a church title of "intercessor" or "minister." In fact, you can have all the titles you want, but you will not truly be free to serve the God of the tabernacle unless you are continually cleansed, clothed, and furnished in the way He has appointed.

> The floor of the holy place is a threshing floor, where you have been separated unto His presence.

Behind the second curtain was a room called the Most Holy Place, which had the golden altar of incense and the gold-covered ark of the covenant. This ark contained the gold jar of manna, Aaron's staff that had budded, and the stone tablets of the covenant.

—HEBREWS 9:3–4, NIV

> **The ark represents the human heart, the place where the glory of God can take up residence and transform everything around you.**

LEVELS OF GRACE

As a result of learning to stay in the presence of the Lord, you will experience more changes. Sometimes He may rebuke you or chastise you to correct you. This will bring you into a new level of His grace.

God wants you to grow through every level of the manifestation of His grace. At first, your experience of His grace was limited to receiving His pardon when you fell into habitual sins. As you grow more mature, you move beyond those temptations. You will choose to put the needs of others above your own fleeting pleasures. You will truly be able to live behind the veil. There, you will notice whatever is not quite aligned with Him.

> God wants you to grow through every level of the manifestation of His grace.

Too many believers don't understand what going behind the veil means. It's not just the occasional time when you feel deeply moved by God's Spirit. Going behind the veil is not a onetime event or experience—*it is a supernatural lifestyle*. Here, in the holiest place, you will want to hold precious only the things that are in God's heart. Here you will be able to experience His mighty power.

Going behind the veil is not a onetime event or experience—it is a supernatural lifestyle.

How much more, then, will the blood of Christ, who through the eternal Spirit offered himself unblemished to God, cleanse our consciences from acts that lead to death, so that we may serve the living God!

—HEBREWS 9:14, NIV

WILL YOU CARRY THE MANTLE OF PRAYER?

*C*an you trust God enough to obey Him at every level, so that you can meet Him in the most holy place and carry the mantle of prayer to this generation?

Jesus is saying to you, "Come after Me so that I can get rid of everything I see in you that doesn't match the principles of My kingdom." Jesus did not save you so that you could go to church and sit in a pew or sing in the choir. He didn't bring you into the kingdom of God so that you could have a "Christian experience." He brought you into His heavenly realm so that you could become a "fisher of men."

> Jesus brought you into His heavenly realm so that you could become a "fisher of men."

The place of prayer, the threshing floor, is where you will receive your spiritual assignment—and the power to walk it out.

When Jesus called the disciples, they immediately left their fishing nets and followed Him. In other words, they walked away from their own abilities and submitted to Lord to lead them on the unknown path ahead. From that day forward, they walked in the reality of true intimacy with the Lord.

———※ ✦ ※———

The place of prayer, the threshing floor, is where you will receive your spiritual assignment—and the power to walk it out.

———※ ✦ ※———

Come after Me and be My disciples, and I will make you to become fishers of men. And at once they left their nets and [yielding up all claim to them] followed [with] Him [joining Him as disciples and siding with His party].

—MARK 1:17–18

STEP BY STEP

*W*hen Jesus calls you to *salvation*, it speaks of the outer court. When He calls you to *discipleship*, it relates to the holy place, the place of maintenance. But when He calls you to your divine assignment as a *fisher of men* (an intercessor), He wants you to develop spiritual disciplines, which include maintaining the anointing, keeping oil in the lamp, putting fresh bread on the table, and refreshing the coals on the altar.

Unless you possess these elements, you will not be able to hear what He hears, see what He sees, and know what only He knows. You cannot become an effective fisher of men until you drop your own net!

> God wants you to develop spiritual disciplines.

Drop what you think your ministry is supposed to look like, and give it all to Jesus. Abandon your claims. You have received the highest call in God's kingdom, the call to effectual, fervent prayer. Live a submitted life, so that your prayers will not be empty. Don't carelessly confront the enemy and say, "I command you, Satan…" until you know you are established in the power and the character of God.

Live a submitted life so that your prayers will not be empty.

To what purpose is the multitude of your sacrifices to Me [unless they are the offering of the heart]? says the Lord. I have had enough of the burnt offerings of rams and the fat of fed beasts [without obedience]; and I do not delight in the blood of bulls or of lambs or of he-goats [without righteousness]. Bring no more offerings of vanity (emptiness, falsity, vainglory, and futility); [your hollow offering of] incense is an abomination to Me.

—ISAIAH 1:11, 13

FROM THE THRESHING FLOOR

When King Solomon brought the ark of the covenant into the new temple, the glory of the Lord filled that place until the priests could not remain standing to minister. (See 1 Kings 8:5–11.) You will find that something inside you wants to lie prostrate whenever you are in the presence of the glory of God. You will want to lie down on the floor, like all the angels and saints do before the throne of God in heaven.

All living creatures fall on their faces to worship Almighty God. We are certainly no exception. We respect the fact that we are not equal to His glory, and we lower ourselves to the lowest possible position.

You can pray in any position—kneeling, standing, walking, lying down on your back—but in the place of deepest prayer (the threshing floor) none compares to facedown on the floor.

Stretch yourself out. Lie at His feet. It is the best position for communing with Him.

You can pray in any position—kneeling, standing, walking, lying down on your back—but in the place of deepest prayer (the threshing floor) none compares to facedown on the floor.

A vast host…stood before the throne and before the Lamb…and all the angels were standing round the throne and round the elders [of the heavenly Sanhedrin] and the four living creatures, and they fell prostrate before the throne and worshiped God. Amen! (So be it!) they cried. Blessing and glory and majesty and splendor and wisdom and thanks and honor and power and might [be ascribed] to our God to the ages and ages (forever and ever, throughout the eternities of the eternities)!

—REVELATION 7:9, 11–12

THE PURPOSE OF THE THRESHING FLOOR

What does the threshing floor really represent? We see several examples of threshing floors in the Old Testament, two of which are the settings of powerful breakthroughs—for King David and for Ruth.

David purchased a threshing floor from Araunah the Jebusite and made sacrifices of repentance that stopped a plague that had killed 70,000 Israelites. His son Solomon later constructed his temple in that location. (See 2 Samuel 24:18; 2 Chronicles 3:1.)

In the story of Ruth and Boaz, Ruth symbolizes the church, and Boaz symbolizes Jesus Christ. Ruth, in obedience to her mother-in-law, washed and prepared herself and then went in to the threshing floor (the intimate place of Boaz) to seek his favor, lying prostrate at his feet. In return, he covered her with his mantle. (See Ruth 3:1–7.)

In the same way as David and Ruth, we can obtain God's powerful intervention on our personal threshing floor. Though the threshing floor in the Old Testament may have been an open field on the far side of the country, God is establishing the idea that wherever you make *your* threshing floor, whatever place has been sanctified for you, you are guaranteed to come out with a victory.

> In the same way as **David** and **Ruth**, we can obtain God's powerful intervention on our personal threshing floor.

Wherever you make your threshing floor, whatever place has been sanctified for you, you are guaranteed to come out with a victory.

Well done, you upright (honorable, admirable) and faithful servant! You have been faithful and trustworthy over a little; I will put you in charge of much. Enter into and share the joy (the delight, the blessedness) which your master enjoys.

—MATTHEW 25:21

Your Threshing Floor Experience

*H*ave you embraced every element in the pattern of prayer as revealed in the tabernacle of the Old Testament? To find out, use this list:

- Have you entered the gate by accepting Jesus Christ as your Savior and Lord?
- Have you passed through the outer court of your initial conversion experience?
- Have you washed at the brazen laver of the Word of God, allowing the Holy Spirit to build godly character in you?
- Have you become a living sacrifice on the brazen altar?
- Do you put on the tunic of righteousness and wear it daily?
- Have you completed your garments with the sash, the robe of blue, the ephod, the breastplate, and the miter so that you can enter God's divine presence?
- Have the ingredients of God's holy anointing oil become part of your life?
- Have you received the divine protection of the spiritual coverings of your tabernacle?
- Have you embraced the power of the contents of the holy place: the table of shewbread, the menorah, the golden altar of incense?
- Have you prostrated yourself on the floor in gratitude, adoration, and pure humility?

> Have you embraced every element in the pattern of prayer as revealed in the tabernacle of the Old Testament?

Now your intercession, empowered and directed from His divine presence, will shatter the gates of hell. Having followed Him all the way to the holy place behind the veil, the impossible not only becomes possible—*it becomes reality.*

In the holy place behind the veil, the impossible not only becomes possible—it becomes reality.

Behold, I will make you to be a new, sharp, threshing instrument which has teeth; you shall thresh the mountains and beat them small, and shall make the hills like chaff. You shall winnow them, and the wind shall carry them away, and the tempest or whirlwind shall scatter them. And you shall rejoice in the Lord, you shall glory in the Holy One of Israel.

—ISAIAH 41:15–16